THE BIG BOOK OF
HEALING DRINKS

Juices, Smoothies, Teas, Tonics, and Elixirs to Cleanse and Detoxify

FARNOOSH BROCK

Skyhorse Publishing

Skyhorse Publishing books may be purchased in bulk at special discounts for sales promotion, corporate gifts, fund-raising, or educational purposes. Special editions can also be created to specifications. For details, contact the Special Sales Department, Skyhorse Publishing, 307 West 36th Street, 11th Floor, New York, NY 10018 or info@skyhorsepublishing.com.

Skyhorse® and Skyhorse Publishing® are registered trademarks of Skyhorse Publishing, Inc.®, a Delaware corporation.

Visit our website at www.skyhorsepublishing.com.

10 9 8 7 6 5 4 3 2 1

Library of Congress Cataloging-in-Publication Data is available on file.

Cover design by Abigail Gehring
Cover images courtesy of www.istockphoto.com

Print ISBN: 978-1-5107-4212-3
Ebook ISBN: 978-1-5107-4213-0

Printed in China

To all who seek health and healing from Mother Nature

Contents

Acknowledgments

A book is always a team effort and ***The Big Book of Healing Drinks*** was no exception. I'd like to thank **Skyhorse Publishing** and especially **Abigail Gehring** for welcoming another book in the series of ***The Healthy Juicer's Bible*** and ***The Healthy Smoothie Bible***. We're fortunate and delighted to work with this amazing publisher. Next, I'd like to thank my husband and business partner, **Andy Brock**, for helping me both at the whiteboard with brainstorming and in the kitchen with preparations to make our yummy concoctions and document the entire process—and for the love and support along the way. **Christina Canters,** my apprentice in Melbourne, Australia, provided her Turmeric & Ginger Latte recipe which is included in this book, and my fabulous neighbor, **Danielle Carpenter**, was an awesome guinea pig by tasting many of the smoothies, tonics, and juices to give us that third set of impartial taste buds. I'm grateful to my family who is always supportive of all my endeavors. I'm most grateful for you, dear reader, for choosing to heal yourself by establishing better habits and exploring the ideas in this book to help you do that. Thank you.

INTRODUCTION

Embracing the Healing Process

Maybe you are pretty healthy and make reasonably good choices on a day-to-day basis, and yet you feel you could be doing a little *more* for your body. Maybe you are bored with a dull health regimen and want to have more fun as you get healthier and fit. Maybe you have had some kind of health crisis that served as a wake-up call, and now you're ready to take steps toward a healthier lifestyle. Or maybe you are curious about creative ways to make subtle, simple changes in your life that would result in a happier, healthier you! Whatever your reasons may be, you are here because you care about your wellness and well-being and, deep down, you know you can benefit from more vitality, energy, and joy of living.

I wrote this book for you. As someone who has experienced all of the above, I'm always on a quest to make the health journey more fun, creative, easy, and efficient so my health can sustain itself over many long and happy decades. This book isn't a serious lecture on what you should or shouldn't be doing, and it won't give you a regimented diet to follow in order to lose those stubborn last ten pounds. This book is about making our wellness more fun, more creative, more sustainable with our lifestyle, and more rewarding. This book is about falling in love with the process of healing, and maybe, falling in love with yourself and knowing without a shadow of a doubt that you are oh so worthy of having it all.

Definition of Healing in This Book

The book is titled **The Big Book of Healing Drinks** and, before we go further, I'd like to define the word "healing" in the context that we will be using it. We define healing this way: No matter what health state you may be in right now—whether

you are a world-class fitness star or an average individual with normal health numbers, whether you are weak or strong, young or old, a health nut or a health newbie—healing means you will feel better, have more energy, become healthier, be happier, and improve your current state of being. We accomplish this by adding one or more of these healing drinks to your diet regularly and, if need be, eliminating one or more drinks or foods that are poor choices.

Therefore, healing is relative to where you are. Start by defining your own point of reference. You start the healing from there while other readers start at their reference points. Healing will measure how far along you travel from your reference point toward your ideal state of well-being. The healing is always physical and emotional, as everything is connected, and the more healing that you experience on a physical level, the more healing you will experience in your emotional and mental state.

What You Won't Get in This Book

The Big Book of Healing Drinks is not a weight-loss book, although you may very well experience weight loss by taking the healing drinks regularly. It is also not a "cure" anything book, nor do we make any promises to "fix" ailments or health issues for which you need to seek a professional's help. This is also not a diet book, where you get instructions for a strict juice-detox or liquid fasting. This book has 92 original recipes, and yet it is not *just* a recipe book either, as it also discusses habits and mindsets, both of which are essential to the healing process.

I am a voracious reader and my rule of thumb is this: if I can take one single unexpected insight from a book, then it has done its job. May you walk away with many such insights to improve your life and well-being.

Applying the Healing Drinks to Your Goals

Our health is a journey, and it has ups and downs, lows and highs, like any journey worth going on. At every stage of the journey, your goals naturally apply to what you are dealing with at that moment. As I said earlier, this book will have ideas and insights for you on any stage of your health journey. It is up to you to decide what most applies to you and where to best focus your time and energy. For instance, if you are making yourself stronger and healthier, maybe weight loss is not on your radar so much as getting the right nutrients into your body, so perhaps your initial focus would be on meal replacement and high-protein smoothies. But if you're trying to detox and cleanse your body after years of poor habits, then your initial focus may take you straight to the healing juices, teas, elixirs, and tonics in this book.

To help you find the drinks that will apply most to you and your goals, I've listed the top benefits of the drinks in each section. Just read the start of each section and when you find what's most relevant to you, start there. This book is not a novel, so no need to cover it in sequential order!

Inspired Wellness, One Healing Drink at a Time

What if you could build a new foundation of wellness *and* feel inspired to live a healthier lifestyle every time you reach for something to drink? What if you could be mindful and intentional about every beverage, and not in a rigid or regimented way but in an exciting way?

This is an inspired wellness book, and our goal is to offer you the most healing drinks for your body and, as a result, help you experience a clear conscience for your mind. This is a book that will challenge you to think differently about the next beverage you consume. This is a book that will provide you with creative and abundant options as to what to drink to both hydrate and nourish your body, depending on your mood or situation.

The decision to focus on drinks was inspired by the general dietary neglect in this area. The weight-loss and fitness industries focus heavily on food, so the minute you decide to lose a few pounds or to prepare for a new fitness challenge, you probably think about what you're eating. Far less attention goes into what beverages you're consuming.

We start by talking about what to drink and what to avoid. Then we dive into the world of healthy and healing drink choices and walk you through every step on how to plan and prepare and enjoy those drinks. I've explored and experimented with ways to build up these micro-Zen habits, which aim to empower your healing process in a way that is fun, accessible, efficient, and diverse. This book speaks to those ideas and shares those discoveries to help you to easily incorporate *at least* one healing drink into your daily habit of living mindfully.

It Is Never Too Early or Too Late to Start Healing Your Body

Aging is humbling. I laugh when I recall that in my early thirties, when I first got interested in my own health, I felt it was already "a little late" to make any big changes in my life! Now, years later, I firmly believe that it is never too early or too late to start healing your body. As an adult of any age, you can always get healthier, be more aware, make better choices, and create more of a healing environment to house your body and mind. Whether you are in your forties or your eighties, you are still here. You are a living, breathing being, and as long as you are here, you can make changes and take actions that will bear fruit for you. And yet, do not take this as an excuse to procrastinate a minute longer. Here and now is when your healing starts.

Emily Crowell Photography

Health and healing weren't anywhere on my radar in my twelve-plus years in my corporate career. I was too busy rushing after the next plum project or the next impressive promotion at my fancy fast-paced career. It just so happens that I was always reasonably fit, and took decent care of myself, but beyond that, my life focus was forever on external goals and ambitions at the expense of everything else. Over and over again, I'd sacrifice family time, personal relationships, friendships, even my marriage to the benefit of my career.

Then 2007 came, and with it, the hardest year for my family. My dad was diagnosed with advanced stage colon cancer. In the long weeks spent in the ICU for multiple surgeries and complications, followed by months of recovery, I woke up to what mattered. My lofty ambitions lost all their appeal overnight. The desire to climb the corporate ladder was gone instantly and in its place was the deep need to reconnect with my family and with my own health and well-being. In the past years, I had made countless business trips coast to coast, neglecting my health and marriage. Enough was enough. When I paused to see what was happening, I realized that I was depleted. Stress and anxiety had accumulated over the years, and I didn't have the knowledge or the tools to manage these demons in my life. My nutrition had gone downhill as a result of frequent trips without recovery time in between. My exercise habits were nearly non-existent, and my mind had turned into an annoying ticking time bomb, just waiting for excuses to explode at those around me or lash out at the world for all the things that kept going "wrong."

I just wasn't happy and I didn't like who the person I had become.

At the time, I didn't know what I needed to get better, but it was clear that what I was doing wasn't working anymore. Slowly, I began to take the steps toward restoring my health and reconnecting with my mind, body, and soul. In that process, I always turned to the most natural healing methods for support, whether it would be for aches or pains, indigestion, extra weight, anxiety, stress, fatigue, unhappiness, or insomnia. Then, as now, my mantra was to always seek the most natural, medication-free way to heal myself first. This does not mean I mess around when I have an infection or think twice about taking antibiotics prescribed by my doctor. But when medication is optional, which is way more often than we realize, I opt out and seek natural healing.

After my dad's trip to the hospital, I became totally obsessed with green juicing, a journey that ultimately led to the joy of sharing my newfound insights with the publications of **The Healthy Juicer's Bible** and **The Healthy Smoothie Bible**. Juicing and smoothies were two of the many natural healing habits that I've relied on for years, but habits have a funny way of testing us over the long term and, in recent years, I had fallen out of both habits for stretches of time. There's nothing particularly wrong with falling out of habits, I'd remind myself, as long as I'm able to maintain my health at the same level. But that wasn't necessarily the case either. As you know, habits are critical to sticking to your health goals. The more deeply you develop your good habits, the more likely you are to set yourself up for success again and again. But habits lapse if you get complacent. So how do you get back and stay on track? This is an important topic we explore at more length in the Building the Habit chapter (page 187).

In 2017, I made an effort to recommit to my habits, and this time, I wanted to also explore a wider range of healing drinks beyond juicing and smoothies, one that provided a larger variety, more options. With juicing and smoothies as my two main options for healthy drinks, I would sometimes get bored. So I set out to discover more ways to get the complete nutrition my body needs while still having fun in the process. What if I craved a hot drink? What if I had just two minutes to make something? What if I was on the go and needed a portable drink? What if I was really hungry but would rather sip my "food"? What if I wanted something savory? Those are the seeds that planted the idea for this book.

In this book, you will find plenty of healing smoothies and juices, but we also go deeper and wider. We get more creative with our healing drinks. We introduce you to elixirs and tonics and shots. We explore teas and hot water therapy and non-dairy and non-caffeine lattes. We bring you savory filling options with various bone broths. We aim to give you something delicious for all seasons and reasons of your healing. Will you go on the adventure with us?

CHAPTER 1
THE HEALING MINDSET

The healing mindset is a way of being and living with your body that feels good, right, and aligned to your natural state. Your natural state is a state of joy and happiness, peace and harmony. This is home for your body. To get back home and to stay there, you must heal yourself. The healing mindset here gives you the tools and resources to find your way back to this natural state of equilibrium.

Before you start doing anything though, your mind must come on board. Otherwise, you'll be resisting the process all the way! When I teach healing mindset or business mindset to my clients, I make it very clear that there is nothing to do yet. There is only a different way of being with yourself and with the world around you. For instance, if you find yourself to be a victim of circumstance in life, you now want to find yourself as a leader of your life. That requires nothing of you except that you choose to see yourself differently. Or, if you always predict the worst outcome of every situation, you now want to give yourself permission to play with the best possible outcomes. Those are examples of a shift in mindset. You are simply becoming aware of your current state of mind and realizing that this state may not be serving your highest interest, and then exploring a better state of mind that is more useful and beneficial.

As Eckhart Tolle tells us in his beautiful book, *The Power of Now*, "If you get the inside right, the outside will fall into place." So we first have to change our inner state, and that is what I refer to as mindset here.

Rate Your Current Healing Mindset

So what does a healing mindset look like? And how do you know if you already have one or not?

How you feel in your body is the biggest indicator of your health and your mindset.

Your mind has a big effect on your physical self. For instance, if you're eating healthy and exercising and taking care of yourself but you still get down on yourself, criticize your efforts, and think it's just not enough, your mindset is working against you, and you still may not experience well-being in your body. If, on the other hand, you have a weight challenge or are working through a health issue, and yet you are calm and confident that all your work will pay off, and you are staying generally positive, and applauding your self-care efforts, you likely feel well on your way to physical health and well-being.

When your mindset works for you, this is a healing mindset, and this plays a large role in your body's healing as well.

So let's see where you are. Use these questions to give yourself a quick assessment. On a scale of 1–10 where 1 is poorly and 10 is wonderfully, give each question a score. Note: Poorly can be interpreted as fatigue, low on energy, stressed, anxious, unhappy, achy, or sluggish. Wonderfully can be energized, clear in the head, relaxed, focused, content, strong, healthy, vibrant, and happy.

1. How do I feel every morning upon waking up?
2. How do I feel after eating breakfast?
3. How do I feel midmorning?
4. How do I feel after a full day of work and play?
5. How do I feel after my workout or exercise routine?
6. How do I feel in the evenings?
7. How do I feel before sleep?
8. How do I feel overall about my health?

How did you do?

If you had more than four answers with scores between one and five, then your mindset is not contributing to your healing and it may even be a detriment to it. There is much room for you to incorporate more healing in your life and tip the scale to the other side.

If you had more than five or six answers closer to the full ten score, then you are doing wonderfully indeed, and yet, you will find that even you can take your healing to the next level.

The scale is only useful in helping you determine where you're starting from. It is not a score to make you feel good or bad, but simply to make you aware. Remember that! This healing mindset starts and proceeds with positivity all the way.

The most helpful attitude is curiosity. Get curious and wonder why you are not a ten more often than not, which is your natural normal state of existence. In our fast-paced society and our digital age, millions of fun distractions are constantly taking up your time. Healing is about tuning in with your body, slowing down the insane race of life, and having a deeper and healthier relationship with yourself. Yet, that's not the normal flow of work and societal pressures. Still, you're in charge. When you put your own health and well-being first, you will have taken care of your most precious asset. When you feel good, you're best equipped to take care of your life responsibilities such as family, job, parents, pets, hobbies, community, and causes. But when you live a life when your health and well-being are more of an afterthought, you will suffer consequences in all areas of your life.

The priority has to shift first if you want to adopt a true healing mindset.

Why Are You Doing This?

Simon Sinek, the author of the bestselling book *Start with Why* believes the foundation of success in the pursuit of big goals in life is knowing your why. He believes that people and companies must be absolutely clear as to why they are doing what they are doing. Whatever goal or mission you have, he'd ask you to state your why: So why are you pursuing this goal? What does it really mean to you? What is the deep reason that commits you to your goal? Why not pursue another goal instead of this one?

Sometimes we achieve our goals just fine without knowing the crystal clear why behind them. Sometimes, we are so clear why we want something that we don't even need this reminder.

Perhaps you are crystal clear about why you want to heal your body. After all, aren't the obvious reasons—feeling better and improving your lifestyle—enough? Sure. They can be. But if you want to take it even one step further, pause and ask yourself why healing your body at this time and place in your life matters so much. The reward of doing this is that it recommits you to your goal, and it makes your resolve much stronger.

Here are some common whys to healing that my clients have shared with me:

- "I want to have more energy."
- "I want to be a better role model for my children."
- "I want to feel alive more often."
- "I want to have a better relationship with myself, so I can improve my relationship with others."
- "I want to be in a better mood so I like myself more."

- "I want to be free of aches and pains."
- "I want to be around a very long time!"

Spend two minutes to reflect on your why. Write it down. Or say it out loud. Or whisper it to yourself. Just get clarity on your why as you read this book and learn to adopt more of a healing mindset in your life.

Then, when you have your why, smile. This is such good news! When your mind is on board, your body will come along. Your body is so smart. It knows how to heal itself and, with your mind's permission, you are now a united team working together toward a common and beautiful goal. On this healing journey, it is important to set yourself up for success from the start. The healing mindset starts and ends in your mind, in your thoughts, and in the stories you tell yourself, so become more aware and tuned in to what those are, as you learn about new ways to heal your body.

The Power of Small Changes

Sometimes, the smallest changes have the largest impact and sometimes, it takes an outsider to point out our blind spots, obvious as they may be after the fact. Let me share with you my, ahem, very humbling experience not too long ago. Here I was feeling so proud of myself for making all these positive changes in my life and adopting all these great health habits. To name a few, I had established a strong daily home yoga practice. I had explored new eating regimens and settled with the Whole30 way of eating, which helped eliminate my food intolerances and improve my relationship with food. I had given up coffee and adopted a tea drinking habit that has greatly improved my digestion. I stayed far away from alcohol and processed sugars. Seriously, I felt incredible about my lifestyle. But I would have these occasional stomach cramps and finally we decided to go see our family doctor. As always, my husband was also there. The look on my husband's and the doctor's faces when I proudly told them how much water I drank daily—something like 4 cups a day—is imprinted in my mind: It was the look of utter shock.

That's right! Like so many others, I was walking around half-dehydrated, and here I thought of myself as such a health nut! The joke was on me! What a huge blind spot that was. That single insight with a casual doctor visit woke me up and, thankfully, improved everything yet again to a whole new level with just one small change: drinking more water daily. I started a daily regimen of drinking 3 liters of

filtered room-temperature water, which is about 14 cups per day every day, and started to treat this habit as seriously as brushing my teeth. I talk more about how I developed the water drinking habit in the later chapters. Suffice it to say, the stomach pains went away, the cramps disappeared, and my skin started clearing up and glowing even more, and I felt oh so much better. My key takeaway here was this: even though I was truly healthy in many ways, this was a blind spot, and the answer was a simple shift in my routines.

Blind spots are harder for those of us who think we have it all figured out or have a reputation of being healthy. Don't lose sight of the fact that we all have more to learn. What could be a blind spot for you, even if you consider yourself a healthy person?

Small changes can and will have powerful results, so be encouraged. Think of a teeny tiny seed planted into the earth. The changes that seed is undergoing are invisible as far as an outsider can tell, but we know full well that the seed is growing and being nurtured in the dark, damp earth. At first, no one may notice the changes you're experiencing, but if you continue to nurture yourself, not only will the changes become visible, but the growth and beauty you experience will be unstoppable. You are that seed. You are also the one that nurtures and loves the seed until you sprout into the new you.

You don't need to change your whole life regimen in order to feel better or get healthier. This book is not about big changes, which can sometimes feel overwhelming and which often end up making us feel discouraged to the point that we end up doing nothing. This is about how a simple change or a simple shift in daily habits can and will go a long way.

So let's explore and find ways toward teeny tiny shifts on a regular basis to integrate more healing drinks into your daily routine.

The Power of Good Choices

A change in your lifestyle or diet can be exciting and intimidating at first. If you're like me, whenever you decide to make a change, you'll obsess about it for the first few weeks, documenting everything and tracking it in your productivity app. And then, your old habits come calling on you, and inevitably, you slip here and there. If that happens enough times, you'll declare you've "fallen off the wagon" and that you "might as well quit." Most people do quit after that happens, but a few press on. They know from experience that change shakes things up and some things have to move out so that they make room for the new habits to get in.

What would happen if *you* chose to press on instead of giving up after you've fallen off the proverbial wagon of maintaining a healing habit? What would happen if you forgave yourself for "cheating" on the new habit with a time-old habit and got right back to the new habit?

The Soda Saga

Sodas are far from a healthy beverage option by any stretch. They are either loaded with sugar or with chemicals (if you get the "diet" version) and it's been shown in numerous studies that they contribute to weight gain and diabetes and a host of other problems. You can educate yourself more on your particular brand of soda by doing a simple search on respectable medical websites online. For now, let's agree that soda is not good for you and let's say soda is also one of your weaknesses. You've grown up drinking it. It reminds you of good times and sweet memories. Even if you know all the evidence against soda on an intellectual level, if you totally understand that drinking soda regularly is bad for your general health, your brain doesn't care because it has a very strong and special link with soda.

Now say you challenge yourself to stop drinking soda. The logical side of you is on board. Great start! You are motivated. You are determined. You can do this. Then you get invited to a friend's BBQ party and you find yourself saying "yes, please" without a blink of an eye when they offer you a can of your favorite soda. The emotional side takes over. You drink it, pushing the guilt away, and enjoy the rest of the party. The next day, you feel guilty. You broke your pact with yourself, and your inner critic is being loud and obnoxious. That's the category that I coin as "life happens!", acknowledging that what happens next is up to me! As you go through the following day, you get to make new choices. Yesterday's BBQ party is over. The fact that you drank one soda does not mean that you have a "weakness" or "lack of self-control" issue, which is the narrative that comes up for most of us. You simply made a different choice at the BBQ than you would have liked. That choice is entirely independent of the ones you get to make in the starting now. Stop telling yourself, "I always do this! I have no self-control whatsoever!" Not true. Nor is this going to determine the results of your healing journey, because one or even several poor choices over a long period of time are inconsequential. You are building life habits here, and as long as the net result of your choices is a positive, as long as you choose a healing drink over a poor sugary chemical-induced or alcohol-containing drink more often than not, then you, my dear, are going in the right direction. I mean, sure, you can expedite your results by making good choices more frequently, but you are still moving toward healing by every single good choice that you do make.

Remembering this can enable you to easily let go of the "soda incident," even have a good laugh, and then start afresh, making better choices today.

This subtle shift in mindset can be the difference between reaching your healing goals versus straying further from them.

CHAPTER 2
START HERE: HEALING WATER

Drink Your Water. Every Single Day!

We won't list all the crucial reasons that drinking sufficient clean filtered water is absolutely essential to your well-being. I will simply list my favorite reason: The best motivator for drinking more water is for proper and regular elimination of your body waste, a key indicator of your overall health. This particular body function may be one that we'd rather not discuss or think about, but that doesn't change its critical and permanent role in your health. There is a yogic belief in Kundalini yoga, which says that it's not so much the food you consume that matters but rather your body's ability to efficiently and properly digest and eliminate waste. If you don't have regular—as in daily, or at least every other day—elimination, the first place to start is improving the state of the matter is in your hydration. Water is the primary way to hydrate your body.

How much water are you drinking? Actually keep track for a day so that you can't fool yourself into thinking you're drinking more than you are. Water is not very exciting, yet drinking enough of it could be the one change you make that will shower you with wonderful good health.

Drinking more water is not exactly rocket science or a secret, and yet according to *Medical Daily*,[1] up to 75 percent of Americans may be suffering from chronic dehydration. Just because we know better does not mean we do better. Why is it so hard to drink our daily dose of water? According to that same report, you only need to drink ten cups of water per day. That is about 2.35 liters of water. After my doctor visit, I have been drinking a minimum of 3 liters

---

1 Ericson, John. "75% of Americans May Suffer from Chronic Dehydration, According to Doctors," *Medical Daily*, 3 Jul 2013, www.medicaldaily.com/75-americans-may-suffer-chronic-dehydration-according-doctors-247393

every day, and more if I'm particularly active or spend time in the sun. I don't exactly win a medal for it, but the sweet rewards my body gives me from doing *just this one thing* are extremely encouraging. Sometimes, drinking plenty of water is the *only* thing I can do to keep up my health habits, especially when we are on the road and eating poorly or not getting enough rest. The rewards of adequate hydration include the stuff that makes you smile: glowing skin, more energy, better sleep, regular elimination, and more intentional versus impulsive eating. Building your water habit and sticking to it may just be the key to healing yourself.

THE BIG BOOK OF HEALING DRINKS

How Not to Drink Your Water

1. Say no to plastic bottled water.

We don't need a degree in environmental science to know that bottled water is terrible for the environment, and that most bottled water tastes stale and of plastic. No matter if the bottled water companies use BPA-free plastic, if those bottles have been exposed to heat or sit around for a while, some chemicals may still seep into the water. While the studies of plastic bottles and their health impact may be inconclusive at the moment, there is no doubting the environmental impact of plastic bottles. They are terrible for our environment for at least two reasons:

a. They take up landfill space
b. They are made with fossil fuels, which are a finite resource

Plus, bottled water is a complete waste of your money. When filtered properly, tap water is not only safe and practically free, it's delicious and you can feel better about being more responsible with your plastic usage. If you are on the go, you can carry your water in a stainless steel container of your choice, which looks so much nicer than having a plastic bottle in your hands. Anything you can do to reduce your plastic water consumption counts!

2. Don't drink it ice cold.

I have never understood America's obsession with filling up a glass of water with tons of ice. While the contrary effects of drinking volumes of ice-cold water aren't scientifically proven, you may wish to consider switching to cool water or water at room temperature. Ice-cold water can be useful to prevent your body from overheating if you're doing lots of cardio exercise in the heat, but here are some of the negative, albeit unproven, claims against drinking ice-cold water:

- It is not good for your vocal cords. My voice teacher was adamant about not drinking cold water, especially if before a long conversation or a talk.
- It can hurt your teeth, and chewing ice is not good for your teeth.
- It can be hard to swallow if you have a sensitive or inflamed throat.
- It can decrease your heart rate.

Plus, it is much harder to drink 3 liters of water at ice-cold temperature than at room temperature or slightly cooler.

If you generally drink your water ice cold, I'm curious: Do you enjoy drinking your water this cold? Is your body getting all its water needs met that way in an easy and efficient way? I found that this is one of the reasons many people don't drink their allotted water and if you think, "Ah! Ten cups a day is *so much water*! I can't possibly drink that!", the water temperature may have something to do with your difficulty. So, just as an experiment, switch to cool or room temperature water for a while to see how it feels. Let your body decide!

How to Best Drink Your Water

Here's how I drink water. You may prefer different routines, but I'm sharing what I do in case it's helpful. I drink primarily from a 27 fluid ounce stainless steel water bottle. My favorite brand is Klean Kanteen, but there are many on the market. Using the same container helps build the habit. When I travel, I often take the container with me. I drink a full bottle four times a day, roughly at 7 a.m., 11 a.m, 3 p.m., and 7 p.m. I may take anywhere from five to fifteen minutes to drink each container, while engaging in other light activities. I use the Brita to filter our water and store our regular water at room temperature, while also making a pitcher of water with a few thin slices of lemon. At times, I make infused water with other fruits and some herbs. I'm careful not to make the water so acidic that it messes with the natural pH balance of my body, but it is so much easier for me to drink my water with a little natural flavor.

Drinking plain filtered water at room temperature is really best, and that's my husband's go-to method, but do what you can to get the habit going first. My hygienist reminds me during every visit: "Don't forget to drink regular water after you drink your juices or your teas. You need to reset your pH balance and plain water is the only answer!" I'm sure she's right, but for where I'm at right now, having some flavor in the water helps me drink enough of it. If you're drinking your water, even if it's ice cold, purchased in a bottle, or with some natural flavor, you're getting the massive benefits of hydration and that's what matters most. Any refinement is bonus!

The Logistics of Drinking More Water

OK, let's say you are definitely willing to get on the water-drinking bandwagon. Fantastic! Now, simple as it sounds, it does take some planning and forethought to integrate the habit on a daily basis. I am fortunate to have the flexibility of working for myself, so I'm at home and within comfortable distance of bathrooms, as well as able to take breaks anytime from my work to accommodate my water habit. But what if you have a demanding job with meetings and long commutes, or, as my teacher and professor friends tell me, rigid schedules with infrequent bathroom visits? What if you are so busy with being a parent or a caretaker that your own needs come second to those of your loved ones? Well, then you start small and I mean, very small. First, do a quick scan of what you already drink in the course of your day and ask yourself if you're willing to switch any of those drinks for plain water. If yes, great! Next, consider any gaps in your schedule. Where might you have an hour to yourself where you can schedule your water breaks? That's right. You may need to schedule your water drinking just like you would a meeting or an appointment. It is *that* critical, and if you do what your calendar tells you to do, this could be an effective approach.

Or, you may want to play with this next idea, which takes a little more courage. If you're going to be drinking your water, you might as well become an advocate for everyone drinking their water, so you can be a role model. Carry your bottle water everywhere. Tell your coworkers or your family about your intention and watch their reaction. They'll be curious and, if they are, you can encourage them to do the same. Perhaps whatever your circumstances, this transparency and encouragement can build more flexibility into your schedule so you can easily accommodate this habit whilst tending to your other daily responsibilities.

Making the Perfect Infused Water

To make the perfect infused water, you'll need the following:

- A clean water source
- A water filtration process

- A glass jug (no plastic)
- Fresh fruits and herbs

First, decide on your infusion flavor. I keep mine simple with basic citrus fruits such as lemon, lime, or orange, berries such as blueberry or strawberry, and herbs such as mint, rosemary, or basil, as well as cucumber. I also use spices from time to time for fun. I use any combination of these or each of them alone.

Here are some combinations that you may want to try for fun:

- Cucumber + strawberry + mint
- Lemon + raspberry
- Orange + lemon + blueberry
- Fresh lavender + lemon
- Lime + ginger root + basil
- Watermelon + mint
- Lemon + thyme
- Orange + cinnamon stick + cardamom + cloves

To prepare your infused water, fill up your glass jug with filtered water and then add all your ingredients in. Wash but do not peel any of the fruit. The amount of fruit or herb is entirely up to you. Just keep in mind, you don't need much to add flavor to your water. I prefer lightly infused water, so I use four small slices of fruit and a handful of herbs for every gallon of water. You can experiment for yourself. The longer the fruit and herbs sit in the water, the more flavorful your water will be. Citrus fruit are pretty quick to infuse, usually within the hour, whereas berries, herbs, and spices might take longer, up to three or more hours.

After adding all your ingredients, you have two options: leave the water to infuse at room temperature, or put it in the fridge. I've read that it's advisable to put your infused water in the fridge after two to three hours to prevent bacterial growth. I will be honest, I don't follow this advice, because I don't like cold water, so I never put my infused water in the fridge. I keep my jug out all day, but I do make fresh infused water every day. So if I don't finish my infused water by evening, I throw it all out and start fresh the next day.

If you have been generous with the portions of fruit and herbs, it can get pretty fruity after a few hours. I recommend making your infused water daily for best results. If you're in a hurry, you can make it overnight; if you go light on the fruits and herbs and spices, you will have the perfectly flavored water in the morning and throughout the whole of the next day.

But Just Drink Your Water

In the end, what matters is that you drink your water allowance every day. Every. Single. Day. If you like it ice cold, then so be it. If you get used to room temperature water, great. If you prefer bottles over filtered water, that's OK. Water will hydrate you all the same, and along with that daily hydration, you will get the countless benefits of the magical H_2O. Become a water champion for your body's sake!

Pure and Simple: Hot Water Therapy

In the fall of 2017, I stumbled onto the Face Yoga Method by Fumiko Takatsu (https://faceyogamethod.com). Fumiko developed this unique style of facial yoga that promises to keep your skin young and supple through natural daily movements and massages. Step aside face-lifts, face yoga has got you covered. I was instantly attracted to Fumiko for two reasons: I wanted to learn all the secrets to natural beauty from this Japanese woman with glowing skin, and I'm always looking to develop new micro-Zen habits that pay off over the long term.

In addition to teaching the Face Yoga Method in her course, Fumiko shared her top health habits for staying hydrated and beautiful. I was willing to try everything, but when she shared her number one health habit, the one she "cannot live without," I was skeptical at first. In fact, I had a good laugh about it later because my mom had told me about this very habit years ago and I had gently brushed her off, thinking nothing of it. Now, not only am I a raving fan of Fumiko's number one health habit, my goal is to get *you* on board with the idea too. Are you ready? It's so simple: **drink hot water throughout the day.** Not lukewarm water. Not room temperature water. Not hot water with lemon or honey, a common beverage prescribed by doctors for nasal congestion or the flu. Plain hot water.

Weird, I thought. Just plain hot water? How boring! And what does it taste like? I like drinking teas. I like drinking lemon water at room temperature. And fresh home-squeezed juices. Plain hot water didn't really sound attractive. As I looked into it more, I found out this is also an ancient Ayurvedic method that can help aid digestion and help your system work more efficiently. So, I admit, curiosity got the better of me, and one evening, I poured a small glass of hot water out of our water boiler and began to sip. I remember I was standing in the kitchen, and my husband was looking at me, waiting to see my reaction, especially as I was mocking the idea while getting ready to do it! To my surprise, I liked it. I liked it a lot. I love the sheer simplicity of this idea so much.

I'm so happy that I was open and willing to do something that at first sounded silly. That in itself has been a powerful message on the health journey: if at

first something sounds silly or even strange to your preconceived notions of how something should be, that's okay. Try it anyway. Certainly honor your intuition, and if something doesn't feel right, pass it up, but otherwise, try new things. One of my nonnegotiable values is to stay away from face-lifts or laser or Botox or other methods and to still keep myself young looking. If it's natural and sensible, I'm willing to try it. If not, no thank you. What are your nonnegotiable values?

Since early 2017, when I picked up this hot water drinking habit, which I absolutely adore, I've experienced wonderful benefits. Based on my own experience and research, the top five benefits of drinking hot water regularly throughout the day are:

1. **Glowing Skin:** I know, I know. This is such an overused promise in every beauty ad under the sun, but it's true. Your skin begins to glow when you drink plain hot water regularly.

2. **Better Digestion:** Hot water helps with digestion and makes it easier for the body to eliminate waste. If you drink hot water with a meal, not only does it encourage you to eat more slowly as you sip away, it also helps your body digest the food more easily.

3. **Calms the System:** There's something calming and grounding about drinking hot water sip by sip. You can feel it relaxing your central nervous system. When you sip your caffeinated drinks, as much as I love mine, and I'm guessing you may love yours, any calmness is intermingled with the stimulation from caffeine. With hot water alone, it's just you and calmness.

4. **It's Easily Portable:** You can take this habit anywhere and be able to keep it up. It's always a plus when habits are portable. When we traveled to Vienna

and Prague in November of 2017, I was so content. In the past, I was always looking for places that would have my type of tea, often to no avail. With the hot water habit as a great go-to option for hot beverage, I could go to any café or restaurant in Vienna or Prague and be certain that they could always accommodate me!

5. **Less Caffeine:** If you consume caffeine regularly in your go-to drink, replacing even one cup with just hot water will lessen your caffeine consumption without much effort on your part. I find that often we want the comfort of a hot beverage even more than what is actually contained in the said beverage. And who knows? You may like it so much that you get your caffeine habit under control. For a while there, I was going overboard with my Earl Grey consumption, and then I realized it wasn't so much that I needed the caffeine—none of us really "need" the caffeine, but that's another discussion—it was that I needed the comfort of holding a hot familiar drink which I could sip as I worked.

There Is Hot Water and Then, There's Hot Water

I may not be able to dictate the preparation of my hot water when I'm out and about, but at home, here is how I make delicious tasting hot water.

First, I run my tap water through a water filter. Water tastes slightly different depending on your location. I live in the southeastern US; different regions of the world have different waters. I've had the most delicious waters in my life in New Zealand, Scotland, and Norway. These countries, with their low-density population and because they're near lakes and mountains, have delicious tap water and, as a result, anything I made with that water tasted more delicious than what I made at home. If you live in any of these places, I'm jealous. But still, that's where home water filters come in. Brita is my favorite way to filter water to improve the taste. We don't have a built-in filter on our tap water; but you can certainly choose to get one installed. As long as you have a filter to remove the health contaminants from your water, it can improve on the taste dramatically. After filtering your water, you need a way to bring it to a boil. You can use a kettle, which is standard and does the job, but it's far from efficient, and you want to set your hot water system up for frequent use here. If you had to boil hot water every time you wanted to drink some, you would simply not do it as often and the habit wouldn't form. If you can invest in something that makes it easier, I highly recommend what we discovered on our first trip to Japan in 2004: a Zojirushi water boiler (or similar brand). The brand is mostly known for their rice cookers, which is what comes up when you first Google them, but this company makes a product called a hot water dispenser and it is the most genius and useful appliance in our kitchen. It has hot water ready to go for you all the time!

What You Pour It In Matters

Always drink your hot water in a glass (making sure it's the type of glass that can withstand hot water) or in china or porcelain cups or pottery mugs. Mason jars are out of the question as boiling water may shatter them! The temperature of your hot water is so that you can only sip it, not gulp it. Pour a cup of boiling water in a cup, let it sit for a couple of minutes, and then start sipping. As much as you can, steer away from drinking from paper cups or mugs used for other drinks with leftover odors of coffee or other beverages. In fact, it's not crazy to have a special hot water drinking glass or cup set aside. I do!

Hot Water Plus a Little Something Extra

On certain occasions, you may want to add to your plain hot water, and while the list of ingredients is endless, my top two recommendations are below:

1. **Hot Water and Mint:** If I have an upset stomach, I add fresh mint leaves to my tea. For years, I had my own mint plant on the balcony, and it produced three varieties of mint, but at some point I got a little lazy about caring for it, and now the local grocer is my mint supplier. Fresh mint goes a long way in healing an upset stomach. I add anywhere from five to seven leaves to a glass of hot water, and sip on it, and then chew the mint leaves. The hot water will turn a light greenish color in less than five minutes, but it doesn't get too strong, as long as you drink it in about fifteen minutes.

2. **Hot Water and Lemon and Honey:** A well-known remedy even recommended by most doctors these days, lemon and honey water is wonderful for combating the symptoms of the common cold. I recommend using only fresh-squeezed lemon and raw honey for best results. Add a half of a small lemon's juice and a teaspoon of honey and drink up. This is such a soothing drink when you are under the weather, but it has benefits even when you're not fighting a cold such as boosting your immune system, maintaining the pH balance of your body, acting as a milk detox, cleansing the liver, and even helping with joint and muscle pain, among others. If you're considering giving up tea, this can be a great way to transition away from your daily cuppa!

CHAPTER 3
HOMEMADE MILKS AND NUT BUTTERS

In this chapter, we explore making the essential bases such as nut liquids, nut butters, and coffee cubes, all of which can be used toward making your delicious smoothies and your non-dairy lattes. We've kept it simple as far as nut milks go, but you can always substitute your favorite nut milk in place of the one called for in the recipe.

For coconut water, I recommend any brand that has pure coconut water made from young, green coconuts with no additional ingredients. My absolute favorite brand in the US is C2O coconut water, original flavor, in the paper carton, not in the can. When I went on my tasting tour of all the popular coconut water brands, C2O was the one I liked best, followed closely by Harvest Bay. Many brands are too sweet, have additional ingredients, or just taste awful. In Canada, there's a brand of coconut water by the name of King Island, and I've never tasted anything as delicious. If you live in Canada, that's your go-to brand and I'm a little jealous!

We have not used any dairy bases such as yogurt or animal milk in the recipes. If you are lactose intolerant or have a sensitive stomach, as do many people, you won't be getting much healing from adding dairy into your smoothies. The nut milks are a safer and, if I may say so, more delicious, option with more benefits and less problems for your gut. If you're used to adding regular milk and/or yogurt to your smoothies, I get it, because I used to love adding yogurt to mine ages ago, but I encourage you to at least *try* a non-dairy milk for a change. Then see how you feel after your healing drink of choice as compared to when you would have one with dairy and yogurt. Even if you're not lactose intolerant, there are benefits to non-dairy milks. Habits are hard to break, but that's what you're here for. I really encourage you to move away from using a dairy base as you build that next smoothie or latte.

Nutritional Information

You will notice that we have included nutritional information for the homemade milks and nut butters as well as the smoothies in the following chapters. We had overwhelming feedback in **The Healthy Smoothie Bible** to include this type of information with recipes for helping the user better plan their caloric intake. While this information is at your disposal here, we do not recommend that you make your decisions based solely on calorie counts. The benefits of the fruits, vegetables, herbs, seeds, nuts, and superfoods should be considered. If you're consuming really high quality ingredients, you may not need to consume as much to feel satisfied, and therefore will be less likely to take in too many calories.

Having said that, do keep this one point in mind: the nut and seed milks discussed in the next section are delicious and packed with nutrients, much more so than the watered-down packaged versions you can buy in the store. However, as nuts are calorie and nutrient dense, they can be a little overpowering when added to a smoothie, which already has fruits/vegetables/nuts/protein powders or any combination of those ingredients. Also, the calories of homemade nut milks can add up quickly. So we recommend that if you're using a homemade nut milk as the base of your smoothie, dilute it with water in a 1:1 ratio (nut milk: water). This will still give you a delicious smoothie and make your homemade nut milks last even longer!

What Are the Best Nut Milks?

I've tried many nut milks over the years, and kept coming back to Califia's unsweetened original or vanilla flavored almond milks. Califia is on the more expensive side of nut milks, and I was okay with that and loved it until my husband started making homemade nut milks, particularly cashew milk and almond milk. After tasting a real homemade nut milk, I've crossed over a threshold and just can't go back to Califia. You may just experience that too when you taste your own homemade milk!

Why do we prefer homemade? Often, this is a choice of economy; it's generally cheaper to make your own homemade anything. In the case of nut milks, if you go for organic, raw nuts, you may find that the savings are not significant, and in fact, I read at least one article that argued it was more expensive to make your homemade nut milks. It really depends on the ratio of nuts to water in the brands that you purchase. Some have as little as 2 percent nuts and the rest is water, sugar, and additives, which allows the manufacturer to charge customers a lower price. However, cost aside, this book is about healing your body, and so removing chemicals from your regularly consumed products is a top priority. To that end, you will find that even my beloved Califia has ingredients that I'm not so proud of, and they're the best on the market!

Whether or not it's cheaper to make your own nut milks, you'll find that homemade nut milks have a concentrated fat content, are more filling, creamier, frothier for your "lattes," and mix much better with your ingredients whether you're making a smoothie or a nightcap shot.

So while you can go with store-bought brands—I did for years—it is so very easy to make your own homemade almond milk, and even easier to make the cashew milk, and I promise you that the taste of your creamy, dense, and delicious milk will convince you it's worth it!

You can also make homemade nut butter, though there are loads of great nut butter options available for purchase. We still love and get Costco's Kirkland almond butter; it has no ingredients other than almonds, and it has a smooth and creamy consistency. We use it to supplement what we make at home. If you buy your nut butter, always check the ingredients, as most brands sneak some unhealthy junk into those jars. But if you've never made your very own nut butter, give it a try—you may really enjoy the process and the results! Just ensure the nuts are fresh! If you have the option to buy in bulk, taste one for flavor and texture before purchase.

To make your own nut butter, you'll want a good appliance to grind the nuts up. I recommend one of these three: (1) a high-speed blender, such as the Vitamix (2) a masticating slow juicer such as the Omega juicer, which comes with the right add-on pieces that switch the functionality from juicing to making nut butter, or (3) a high-powered, heavy duty food processor that is at least of medium size (those tiny food processors won't be able to do the job!). Of these, my husband thinks the masticating slow juicer yields the best nut butters.

Cleaning any of these appliances does take a few minutes. You'll want to scoop out all of your nut butter from around the edges of each containers before getting them ready to wash. Most are dishwasher safe so you don't have to do the heavy lifting yourself.

Storing your milks and nut butters is key to making them last longer. I always recommend glass containers with airtight lids. You may store your milk in a glass jug with an airtight lid, and your nut butters can also go in glass jars or glass Tupperware, depending on how much you make. Both homemade nut milks and nut butters are best stored in the refrigerator. Your nut milk will be good for up to two weeks, but of course, it's best to consume it sooner. Your nut butter will keep for up to three months. If you will consume your nut butter in less than two weeks, you can choose to store it in a dry, dark cabinet instead of a fridge.

In this section, we have several recipes for you from our kitchen including a variety of homemade non-dairy milks as well as homemade nut cacao butters and instructions on making coffee ice cubes. Let's have some fun and make some stuff in the kitchen now!

Homemade Cashew Milk

Cashew milk is the easiest and quickest milk to make at home. It's rich, creamy, and delicious, and there is no need to strain it. The nuts dissolve completely and you are done in less than five minutes! Cashews are delicious. They are packed with vitamins E, K, and B$_6$, and minerals such as copper, phosphorus, zinc, magnesium, iron, and selenium, all of which are important for maintaining good bodily functions.

Yields 5 cups

Ingredients

¾ cup soaked unsalted raw or lightly roasted cashew halves

4 cups filtered water

½ teaspoon vanilla extract

½ teaspoon pink sea salt

Instructions

1. Put cashews and 1 cup of filtered water in the Vitamix or your power blender and process 30 seconds, or until all cashews have been liquefied.

2. Add the rest of the ingredients and the rest of the water, then process another 30 seconds.

3. Store your cashew milk in the refrigerator in a glass container with an airtight seal.

Nutrition per cup: 97 Calories, Fat 8g, Carbs (Fiber/Sugars) 5g (1g/1g), Protein 3g

Homemade Almond Milk

Almonds are delicious and provide you vitamin E, copper, magnesium, and loads of protein. They contain high levels of healthy unsaturated fatty acids, along with high levels of bioactive molecules such as fiber, phytosterols, other minerals, and antioxidants. These nutrients can help prevent cardiovascular disease. While you can eat your almonds in raw form, roasted form, or nut butter form, you can also drink it in homemade delicious almond milk form.

Yields 6 cups

Ingredients

1 cup raw, unsalted almonds

5 cups filtered water

1 teaspoon vanilla extract

½ teaspoon sea salt

Nutrition per cup: 98 Calories, Fat 8g, Carbs (Fiber/Sugars) 4g (2g/1g), Protein 4g

Instructions

1. Soak the almonds for one hour in hot water.

2. After one hour, drain and rinse the almonds.

3. Put almonds, 1 cup water, vanilla extract, and salt into the blender.

4. Blend until the almonds have been processed, then slowly add the rest of the water while continuing to blend another 30 seconds.

5. Pour the contents of the blender through a cheesecloth, nut milk bag, or fine sieve set over a bowl. Let the almond milk drain by pressing the mixture or squeezing the nut milk bag to extract as much liquid as possible.

6. Store your almond milk in the refrigerator in a glass container with an airtight seal.

Homemade Chocolate Hemp Milk

Hemp seeds are delicious and rich in healthy fats and essential fatty acids and are a good protein source with high amounts of vitamin E, phosphorus, potassium, sodium, magnesium, sulfur, calcium, iron, and zinc. You can consume hemp seeds in your smoothies or morning bowl of fruit and nuts. Manitoba Harvest is the highest quality provider of hemp seeds. If you like protein powder, I highly recommend Manitoba Harvest as well as Nutiva for hemp protein, which is my favorite protein powder. Now, let's go one step further and use your hemp seeds, also known as hemp hearts, to make your own homemade hemp milk.

Yields 5 cups

Ingredients

½ cup hemp heart seeds
4 cups filtered water
½ teaspoon sea salt
3 pitted dates
1½ tablespoons cacao
    powder

Instructions

1. Soak the hemp heart seeds in hot water for 30 minutes.

2. Drain the hemp hearts, then add them and 1 cup of filtered water into the Vitamix or your power blender and process for 30 seconds or until liquefied.

3. Add the rest of the ingredients and water, then process another 30 seconds.

4. Store your hemp milk in the refrigerator in a glass container with an airtight seal.

Nutrition per cup: 127 Calories, Fat 7g, Carbs (Fiber/ Sugars) 9g (2g/6g), Protein 6g

Homemade Pistachio Milk Recipe

Pistachios are the most popular nut in Iran, my home country where I was born and grew up. Not only are pistachio nuts tasty and fun to eat, they're also very healthy. These delicious nuts are seeds of the Pistacia vera tree and provide you with healthy fats, protein, fiber, and antioxidants. This beautiful green nut makes a yummy snack, and is delicious made into milk.

Yields 6 cups

Ingredients

1 cup raw, unsalted
   pistachios
5 cups filtered water
1 teaspoon vanilla extract
½ teaspoon sea salt

Nutrition per cup:
98 Calories, Fat 8g, Carbs (Fiber/Sugars) 5g (2g/1g), Protein 3g

Instructions

1. Soak the pistachios for 1 hour in hot water.

2. After 1 hour, drain and rinse the nuts.

3. Put pistachios, 1 cup water, vanilla extract, and salt into the blender.

4. Blend until the pistachios have been processed, then slowly add the rest of the water while still blending another 30 seconds.

5. Pour the contents of the blender through a cheesecloth, nut milk bag, or fine sieve set over a bowl. Let the milk drain by pressing the mixture or squeezing the nut milk bag to extract as much liquid as possible.

6. Store your pistachio milk in the refrigerator in a glass container with an airtight seal.

Homemade Cashew Butter

We love making cashew butter. You can use a Vitamix or any high-powered blender or your food processor, and if you don't have either of those, use a masticating juicer with the right components to switch it from juicing mode to nut butter extraction. My Omega juicers all came with that option, as most masticating juicers do.

Yields ⅔ cup

Ingredients

1 cup roasted, unsalted cashews

1 teaspoon melted coconut oil

½ teaspoon vanilla extract

½ teaspoon sea salt

Nutrition per tablespoon:
62 calories, Fat 6g, Carbs (Fiber/Sugars) 3g (0g/0g), Protein 2g

Instructions

Using the blender/food processor method:

1. Mix all ingredients into your blender or food processor and process until combined and creamy.

2. Pour into an airtight glass container and store at room temperature.

Using a masticating juicer method:

1. Run just the cashews through the juicer three times until a fine cashew meal is produced. We repeat this three times so that the cashews release the oils.

2. Add the melted coconut oil and other ingredients to the cashew meal and mix thoroughly with a spoon.

3. Store in an airtight glass container at room temperature.

Homemade Mixed Nut Butters

Even as we are being good to our bodies, we want to have fun. Enter cacao and raw honey! These two are delicious and nourishing ingredients and you can get creative with them without feeling guilty. So we got a little playful with these two homemade nut butters below. We chose our favorite three nuts: macadamia, Brazilian, and cashews. Any mix of your own favorite nuts will do fine as long as you use 3 cups in total.

Brazilian-Cashew-Macadamia Nut Butter

Yields 2 cups

Ingredients

70g cacao bar

1 tablespoon coconut oil

1 cup salted macadamia nuts

1 cup Brazilian nuts

1 cup cashew nuts

1 tablespoon raw, unprocessed honey

Nutrition per tablespoon: 83 Calories, Fat 7g, Carbs (Fiber/Sugars) 4g (1g/1g), Protein 2g

Almond & Macadamia Nut Butter

Yields 2 cups

Ingredients

70g cacao bar

1 tablespoon coconut oil

1½ cups salted macadamia nuts

1½ cups unsalted almonds

Nutrition per tablespoon: 88 Calories, Fat 8g, Carbs (Fiber/Sugars) 4g (2g/0g), Protein 2g

Instructions for both recipes:

1. Fill a pot with one inch of water and bring it to a gentle boil.

2. Put the cacao bar and coconut oil into a heat-proof bowl, then set bowl over the pot of boiling water, creating a double boiler. Make sure the bowl completely covers the pot so that the steam gently melts the cacao bar and coconut oil.

3. Process the nuts in a food processor until they form a thick paste.

4. Scrape the nut mixture into a bowl, then add the melted cacao/coconut oil mixture.

5. For the Brazilian-Cashew-Macadamia nut butter, add the honey to the bowl at this stage.

6. Mix thoroughly and store in an airtight glass container in a cool location such as your cabinet.

Fortified Homemade Milks in 30 Seconds

For a quick, nutrient-packed snack, I love fortifying my almond or cashew milk with some turmeric or matcha or raw honey, but none of these highly nutritious ingredients dissolve easily in a cup of cold milk right out of the refrigerator, and when you have just two minutes, you can't be bothered with taking out the blender. I love this idea my husband came up with recently.

Turmeric Base:

1 tsp turmeric powder

¼ cup hot water

Matcha Base:

1 tsp matcha tea powder

¼ cup hot water

Liquid Honey Base:

1 tbsp raw, unprocessed honey

1 tbsp hot water

Instructions for all three recipes:

1. Stir ingredients together until the powders are totally liquefied. Then pour them into a small airtight glass container and let cool to room temperature. You can keep them in the fridge for up to three weeks.

2. When you are ready to use them, add 1 tablespoon of your Turmeric Base or Matcha Base or Liquid Honey Base to 1 cup of your milk of choice. Stir it in and enjoy! Et voilà!

Coffee Ice Cubes

I'm not a coffee drinker anymore. In 2007, I gave up my espresso habit, started drinking teas, and have never looked back. The coffee craving eventually left my taste buds for good and I don't miss it at all. Then my husband, the real coffee aficionado in the family, made these coffee ice cubes as we were experimenting with new recipes for this book and asked if he could include a few recipes with coffee cubes. Sure, I said, thinking, but I won't be tasting them.

Boy, was I wrong! Coffee cubes give smoothies a delicious flavor. If you fancy just a little caffeine with some nutrition in your morning drink, the coffee cubes are definitely the way to go. You'll get your breakfast and your beverage in one go! For recipes that include coffee cubes, see the Healing Smoothies chapter (pages 80–105).

To make coffee cubes:

1. Start with your favorite, preferably organic, brand of coffee beans.

2. Grind beans and brew your coffee as you normally would.

3. Let brewed coffee cool to room temperature.

4. Pour into ice cube trays and freeze completely.

5. Keep in the freezer for up to a month. If you don't use them, make a fresh batch.

CHAPTER 4
HEALING JUICES

Benefits of Juicing

A green juice is a nutrient-dense low-fiber drink, which you can only make by using a juicer. I define green juice not so much by the color of the drink, although you will make lots of green-colored juices. Rather, I define green juice as one that contains at least one vegetable in it. All of the healing juice recipes in this section are green juices.

Juicing was my first love in this healing journey. Preparing and drinking fresh juices always makes me feel aligned to the natural state of health and vibrancy. Here are the top ten highlights of why juicing rocks your health. Juicing, when done with the right vegetables and fruits, is a miracle in a glass because a fresh juice:

1. Is a delicious and guilt-free drink.
2. Is a quick way to get your phytonutrients from vegetables and fruits.
3. Gives you an immediate kick of energy.
4. Cleans out your digestive system.
5. Curbs your appetite for junk food.
6. Helps you sleep better.
7. Calms your nervous system.
8. Regulates your body's functions.
9. Eases the detoxification process in the body.
10. Makes you refreshed and rehydrated.

There! More than enough reasons to make it a regular habit. The healing juices in this book always contain one or more vegetables. It is the vegetables—

particularly the leafy greens—that deliver the most benefit to you. The primary reason we add the fruits is to sweeten the juices and make them delicious, though fruits do contain many important vitamins, too.

The two things you will need for proper juicing as far as kitchen equipment goes are a proper juicer and glass containers with airtight lids in which to store your delicious homemade juice. I highly, *highly* recommend a masticating juicer over a centrifugal one. The difference in price is an investment that 100 percent pays off in both the quality and taste of your juice as well as the efficiency of extracting every ounce of juice from your fruits and vegetables. The centrifugal juicer wastes so much produce; your fruit and vegetable pulps are practically soaked in their own juice. It almost hurts to discard so much goodness. My favorite brand of juicer is any model of the Omega juicer, and that has been the case for the past twelve years. I've owned two Omega juicers, though I didn't really need to buy the second one because the first one would refuse to break! All of Omega's masticating juicers will last you years and withstand much juicing.

In the recipe section that follows, you will find that some of the juices contain only three or four ingredients while others may use as many as ten. One preparation tip that I find most helpful is to plan in advance for up to three juice recipes, and then buy all the ingredients at once and store them in the fridge, with a plan to make all three juices in the following three days. While it's best to drink your freshly squeezed juice immediately, it's not always practical with a busy life. If you use a masticating juicer, which slowly extracts the raw juice from your fruits and veggies, as well as a glass—not plastic!—container with an airtight lid, you can store your juice in the refrigerator for up to a week. While the potency may decrease over the course of a week, it's still good for you, and it does not spoil within this time frame. This helps you develop a more regular habit of juicing by making the whole process more manageable.

If you find that you want to go deeper into your juicing journey, you will find more in-depth insights about the benefits and know-how of juicing and even building your own juice recipes from scratch in my first book, **The Healthy Juicer's Bible**.

Now, ready to juice? Onto the recipes we go.

Start with Healing Juices

In this section you will find twenty-three healing juice recipes. Get your juicer ready and get out your glass containers. You will find the recipes with the least number of ingredients listed first. If you are in a bit of a dash, or are craving a simpler taste with fewer ingredients, start there. As you keep going, you will see that you will need more ingredients for the more potent juices.

Quick Preparation Tips

- Wash all fruits and vegetables.
- Check to see if anything needs peeling and do that first. If an ingredient doesn't say "peeled," no need to peel.
- Cut up everything to the size of your chute.
- Run all ingredients in the juicer in whatever order is easiest.
- If you're making multiple juices, run some water through your juicer in between recipes.

Substitution and Addition Guidelines

- You can add ginger or turmeric to just about any juice, or leave them out or use smaller amounts if the flavor is too strong for you. Note that for these roots, we call for "one small chunk." If you've never used ginger or turmeric, start with a ½-inch fresh root and add more as you adapt to the taste.
- You can replace lime for lemon or vice versa.
- You can tone down the leafy green taste of kale by using spinach or, if you want a stronger leafy green flavor, replace spinach for kale or Swiss chard.
- You can adjust the sweetness by using less or more fruit as need be.

Healing Juice Recipes

Red Hot Love

Yields 2 cups

1 small peeled grapefruit
1 medium beet
3 carrots
Small chunk ginger

Beet and Sweet

Yields 2 cups

1 small beet
1 peeled orange
4 carrots
½ lemon

Green Delight

Yields 2 cups

6 leaves Lacinato (dinosaur) kale
½ bunch parsley
½ Italian cucumber
1 green apple
½ lime

Peachy and Tangy

Yields 2 cups

6 carrots
2 pitted peaches
1 large bell pepper
Small chunk ginger

Pear and Grape Joy

Yields 2 cups

3 stalks celery
½ green pepper
1 cup grapes
½ Italian cucumber
½ pear

Green & Clean

Yields 2 cups

3 stalks fennel, ¼ fennel root
   included
6 leaves Lacinato (dinosaur) kale
1 cup grapes
½ pear
½ green apple

Crown Me Queen

Yields 2 cups

3 broccoli crowns
½ pear
½ green pepper
½ Italian cucumber
½ lime

Potato & Tomato Spice

Yields 2 cups

1 sweet potato, unpeeled

4 carrots

3 Roma tomatoes

½ lemon

Pinch of cayenne pepper

Rocking the Roots

Yields 6 cups

3 medium to large size red beets

2 sweet potatoes

1 lemon

10 carrots

Small chunk ginger

Small chunk turmeric

Green Apple Glee

Yields 3 cups

½ bunch watercress

2 apples

1 cup green grapes

1 English cucumber

½ lime

Cherry Tasty

Yields 3 cups

4 celery sticks

4 carrots

2 parsnips

1 lemon

½ lime

20 cherry tomatoes

Small chunk ginger

Pinch of cayenne pepper

Seriously Detox

Yields 7 cups

10 stalks celery

10 cups spinach

1 large Italian cucumber

1 brunch parsley

4 apples

2 lemons

Small chunk ginger

Small chunk turmeric

Pine for Me

Yields 8 cups

1½ lemons

10 stalks Lacinato (dinosaur) kale

½ bunch parsley

4 Persian cucumbers

10 cups spinach

1 small whole peeled pineapple

Small chunk ginger

Small chunk turmeric

Spa Day at Home

Yields 3 cups

4 carrots

3 parsnips

4 celery

1½ yellow apples

½ lime

⅔ bunch parsley

1 cup green grapes

Ultimate Cleanser

Yields 4 cups

1 lime
1 lemon
2 celery stalks
3 large Roma tomatoes
1 large cucumber
4 stalks curly kale
1 bell pepper
Small chunk ginger
Small chunk turmeric
Handful of mint

Deep Kiwi Green

Yields 3½ cups

4 stalks of Swiss chard
2 endives
4 kiwi
1 cup green grapes
1 lemon
1 English cucumber
1 pear

Cool as a Cucumber

Yields 2½ cups

2 peeled oranges
2–3 stalks kale
½ bunch fresh dill
1 English cucumber
1 cup green grapes
Small chunk ginger

Youth Glow

Yields 2½ cups

1 bunch cilantro
4 cups packed spinach
1 whole lime
1 cup green grapes
2 kiwis
4 Persian cucumbers

Spicy Charm

Yields 3 cups

4 cups spinach
1 Italian cucumber
½ bunch parsley
1 pear
2 small apples
Small chunk ginger
Small chunk turmeric
½ jalapeño pepper without the seeds

Mint Condition

Yields 3 cups

2 pitted peaches
1 cup green grapes
6 cups spinach
1 Italian cucumber
3 stalks celery
½ lime
Handful of mint
Small chunk ginger

Kale to the Rescue

Yields 3 cups

15 strawberries
¼ fennel
5 Persian cucumbers
4 curly kale without stem
½ parsley
1 lemon
Handful of mint
Small chunk ginger

Gingerly Recovery

1 cup white grapes
2 Persian cucumbers
1 small lemon
10 stalks Lacinato (dinosaur) kale
½ bunch parsley
1 cup spinach
Small chunk ginger
½ cup unsweetened coconut water

Butter Me Up

Yields 2 cups

½ English cucumber
1 head of butter lettuce
½ bunch parsley
5 Campari tomatoes
1 whole lemon
Small chunk ginger

CHAPTER 5
HEALING SMOOTHIES

Smoothies are the most popular of all healing drinks because they are so quick and easy to make and the ingredient options are virtually endless. Plus, with smoothies, you get all the fiber from the fruits and vegetables, whereas with juicing, you separate out the fiber—or the pulp—and drink only the juice. The fiber in the smoothie slows down the body's absorption of the nutrients and allows you to stay full longer. Both juicing and smoothies are good for you, and while juicing is ideal for a hydrating drink, smoothies are perfect as meal replacements or a filling or light snack, depending on the recipe you use. Plus, you have loads of options as to how you can construct your own healing smoothie!

I define a green smoothie the same as a green juice: not by the color so much as by it containing at least one vegetable. Healing smoothies, made with highly nutritious ingredients such as you will find in our recipes, promise loads of health benefits. Here are the top ten reasons to sip your healing smoothie:

1. They are a fantastic way to eat more whole foods.
2. They keep you hydrated and satiated.
3. They are easy to digest and take very little energy to consume as there is no chewing involved.
4. They help you with overall regularity.
5. They ensure you are getting your vegetables and fruits.
6. They are an excellent source of fiber.
7. They promote weight loss and curb your appetite.
8. They improve the quality of your cravings from sugary/salty food toward healthier options.
9. They boost your overall immunity.
10. They improve your hair, skin, and complexion.

We have included the most delicious and nutritious recipes here for you to enjoy. We have done months of testing in our kitchen to prepare these special recipes for you based on nutritional content as well as taste. We used everything we've learned over the past ten years of making smoothies on a regular basis, plus we've scoured the web for the best product brands for the superfoods, protein powders, and teas used as ingredients. My husband and my neighbor were very kind guinea pigs, so for most of these recipes we had not one but three people vouch for them.

As you get into the healing smoothie recipes, please remember the golden rule: **your taste buds rule.** Experiment, yes, because you've got to get out of your comfort zone and try new recipes to discover new tastes and combinations that you may very well fall in love with, but also respect that you may just not get on board with a particular taste. I for one don't like chia seeds, even though they are all the rage and have many health benefits. So in these recipes I use hemp seeds or ground flaxseed, but you are welcome to use chia seeds instead if you enjoy them. They are of similar nutritional value and purpose, and are easily exchangeable. As for maca powder, my taste buds simply revolt against it, but it has lots of health benefits and if you like it, by all means, add it to your smoothies. At one time I felt similarly about spirulina, but it has grown on me. You'll need to decide for yourself whether you want to keep a particular superfood or pass it up for an ingredient that suits your preferences better.

You'll notice that the recipes here yield anywhere from 2 cups to 6 cups. Note that the nutritional information gives you the per cup serving details and we recommend that you consume no more than two cups of smoothie for a midday meal or snack and no more than three cups for a meal replacement smoothie. You can easily store the leftover smoothie in a mason jar with a tight lid or another other glass container with an airtight lid. You can store them for up to two days in the refrigerator as long as the smoothie does not contain a lot of citrus ingredients (except lemon or lime). If the recipe calls for orange or grapefruit, please drink it up right away.

You will find more in-depth insights about the benefits and know-how of smoothies in my second book, *The Healthy Smoothie Bible*.

Ready to get energized and alkalized with all the fruit, greens, superfoods, and vegetables that your body needs, and all the delicious flavors that you desire? Let's whip up some smoothies together!

You Have Lots of Options

To honor your taste buds and also to customize the healing drink recipes further and perhaps save you an extra trip to the local grocery store, here are some easy substitutions you can make while still keeping the integrity of the original recipe intact.

1. **Chard or kale or collard greens for spinach**: You really can't taste spinach in a smoothie. So if you want a more earthy taste or you want to *know* your greens are there by tasting them, go for chard or kale or collard greens. Leave out the stems though.

2. **Zuchinni or avocado for banana or mango or pineapple**: If you are limiting your fructose intake for any reason, but still want the creaminess in your smoothie, then you can replace bananas or mangos or pineapples with zucchini and/or avocado.

3. **Any nut butter for almond butter or other nut butters the recipe calls for**: Feel free to use your nut butter of choice. Any nut butter will work. We did not use nor recommend any peanut butter as many have allergies to peanuts and the health benefits of almonds, cashews, Brazilian, and macadamia nuts far outweigh those of the peanuts . . . and, if we want to get technical about it, peanuts are a legume, not a nut.

4. **Chia seeds for hemp hearts:** Like I mentioned, I don't have chia seeds in any of the recipes. I use mostly hemp hearts and sometimes ground flaxseed. But you can substitute chia seeds without altering the taste of the recipes by much.

5. **Nut milk of choice for almond or cashew milk:** We've stuck mainly with homemade almond milk and cashew milk when we have used a nut milk

as a base. You can always go with your favorite. I don't recommend soy-based products. However, quinoa milk, rice milk, or coconut milk could be fair substitutions. As always, we highly recommend the homemade versions whenever possible.

6. **Go for extra protein:** The recommended serving of protein powder is either two or three scoops, depending on the brand. In these recipes, you'll

notice I use one heaping scoop per recipe, even if the recipe makes up to two servings. This is because I find that extra protein tends to make the whole drink taste chalky, even with the best brands. Feel free to experiment here. Also, while we do recommend a select number of brands we have tested, any protein powder that is non-GMO, lactose-free, soy-free, gluten-free, and clean of extra chemicals will work.

7. **Sweeten with an extra date:** You should be able to add a date to just about any recipe, if you want to sweeten it more. It's an easy fruit to keep in your cabinets and it is easy to use—no peeling necessary, just a quick pitting and off you go! By the same token, you can remove the date from any recipe if it's a little too sweet for you.

8. **Berries are interchangeable.** We picked specific berries for each recipe, but if you are in a pinch, remember, berries are berries—tart, delicious, and full of antioxidants. Yes, the taste of the recipe might change slightly, but you'll still get the tangy, sweet taste in. We've used blueberries, raspberries, strawberries, cherries, and açaí berries in these recipes. Feel free to mix it up or add blackberries and goji berries if you like.

Tip: Grate your ginger so that it doesn't end up stringy!

Tip: My favorite brand of coconut water is C2O. Having tasted and studied all major coconut water brands, C2O is made with young coconuts and is the most hydrating and delicious. Coconut water is known for replenishing your electrolytes among other benefits.

Ideas for Additional Ingredients

To fortify your smoothies further, you can safely add any of the following to the recipes listed. I suggest you start with half a serving size to see if you like the taste and flavor. I'd even suggest a quarter of the serving if you've never tried the item, and then building from there.

- A plain flavor protein powder
- Chia seeds
- Pumpkin seeds
- Ground flaxseed
- Maca powder
- Goji berries
- Lucuma
- Bee pollen
- Camu camu

SIMPLE GREEN SMOOTHIES WITH ONLY FRUITS AND VEGETABLES AND A WATER BASE

Mango Crush

Yields 3 cups

1 cup fresh spinach

1 cup kale, stems removed

1 frozen peeled banana

1 cup frozen peeled mango pieces

1 cup filtered water

Nutrition per cup: 86 Calories, Fat 0g, Carbs (Fiber/Sugars) 21g (3g/13g), Protein 3g

Orangey Boost

Yields 3 cups

2 cups fresh spinach

1 cup celery

1 frozen peeled banana

1 peeled orange

1 cup filtered water

Nutrition per cup: 68 Calories, Fat 0g, Carbs (Fiber/Sugars) 16g (3g/10g), Protein 2g

The Green Hulk

Yields 2 cups

1 cup fresh spinach
1 cup fresh parsley
1 small Persian cucumber
½ pear (de-cored)
½ peeled avocado
1 cup filtered water
Few ice cubes
Optional: 1 date, pitted

Nutrition per cup: 104 Calories, Fat 5g, Carbs (Fiber/Sugars) 14g (6g/5g), Protein 2g

Popeye Shake

Yields 2 cups

2 cups fresh spinach
½ cup fresh parsley
1 frozen peeled banana
½ cup peeled mango
1 cup filtered water
Optional: 1 teaspoon grated
  fresh ginger

Nutrition per cup: 93 Calories, Fat 1g, Carbs (Fiber/Sugars) 23g (3g/14g), Protein 2g

Simply Creamy

Yields 2 cups

1 cup fresh kale
1 Persian cucumber
½ peeled avocado
1 peeled orange
1 cup filtered water
Few ice cubes

Nutrition per cup: 123 Calories, Fat 6g, Carbs (Fiber/Sugars) 17g (7g/7g), Protein 3g

Fitness Fuel

Yields 5 cups

2 cups spinach

½ medium peeled avocado

1 cup frozen peeled pineapple

1 peeled orange

1 teaspoon grated fresh ginger

2 cups filtered water

Nutrition per cup: 52 Calories, Fat 2g,
Carbs (Fiber/Sugars) 8g (2g/5g), Protein 1g

Zucchini Date

Yields 6 cups

1 cup zucchini

½ peeled avocado

1 cup frozen peeled pineapple

1 cup frozen pear

1 pitted date

2 cups filtered water

Nutrition per cup: 63 Calories, Fat 2g,
Carbs (Fiber/Sugars) 12g (3g/9g), Protein 1g

BREAKFAST FUEL AND
MEAL REPLACEMENT SMOOTHIES

Protein Morning

Yields 4 cups

⅓ cup gluten-free oats soaked
for at least 8 hours in 1 cup
unsweetened vanilla almond milk

1 cup almond milk (in addition to
the almond milk the oats were
soaked in)

1 heaping scoop Naked Pea protein
powder

4–5 coffee cubes

½ cup frozen blueberries

½ frozen peeled banana

1 pitted date

Optional: Fresh mint to taste

Optional: 1 cup fresh spinach

Nutrition per cup: 139 Calories, Fat 3g,
Carbs (Fiber/Sugars) 17g (3g/8g),
Protein 12g

Cacao and Cashew Twist

Yields 3 cups

⅓ cup oats soaked for at least 8 hours in 1 cup unsweetened almond milk

½ cup unsweetened almond milk (in addition to the almond milk the oats were soaked in)

½ cup water

½ teaspoon cacao nibs

1 pitted date

2 cups fresh spinach

1 tablespoon cashew butter

1 teaspoon Matcha tea by Numi

Nutrition per cup: 164 Calories, Fat 9g, Carbs (Fiber/Sugars) 18g (3g/6g), Protein 4g

My Morning Coffee

Yields 3½ cups

⅓ cup oats soaked for at least 8 hours in 1 cup unsweetened almond milk

1 tablespoon Manitoba Harvest hemp seeds

5 coffee cubes

1¼ cup unsweetened almond milk

½ cup frozen blueberries

⅓ peeled avocado

1 pitted date

1 teaspoon coconut flakes

1 tablespoon cashew butter

Nutrition per cup: 170 Calories, Fat 9g, Carbs (Fiber/Sugars) 18g (4g/6g), Protein 5g

Rocket Fuel

Yields 3½ cups

1 frozen peeled banana
½ cup frozen blueberries
½ cup frozen raspberries
5 coffee cubes
1 scoop Nutiva hemp protein
½ cup fresh aloe vera gel
1 pitted date
1 teaspoon cacao powder
1 cup unsweetened almond milk
½ cup filtered water

Nutrition per cup: 85 Calories, Fat 2g, Carbs (Fiber/Sugars) 18g (4g/11g), Protein 3g

Matcha Made in Heaven

Yields 4½ cups

⅓ cup gluten-free oats soaked for at least 8 hours in 1 cup cashew milk
½ cup cashew milk (in addition to the cashew milk used to soak the oats)
2 celery stalks
2 scoops protein powder
1 tablespoon almond butter
1 teaspoon matcha tea powder
4 medium-size frozen figs
⅓ cup pomegranate seeds

Nutrition per cup: 163 Calories, Fat 5g, Carbs (Fiber/Sugars) 22g (4g/12g), Protein 10g

COCONUT WATER–BASED SMOOTHIES

Immunity Boost

Yields 4 cups

½ peeled mango (about 1 cup)

2 cups spinach

1 small cucumber

1 small peeled orange

1½ cups pure, unsweetened coconut
   water

Few ice cubes

Nutrition per cup: 69 Calories, Fat 0g,
Carbs (Fiber/Sugars) 17g (2g/14g),
Protein 1g

Cool Island Breeze

Yields 6 cups

2 cups unsweetened coconut water

6 kale leaves

1 cup grapes

½ green pepper

½ peeled avocado

½ green apple

1 tsp grated fresh ginger

a touch of fennel

4 ice cubes

Nutrition per cup: 129 Calories, Fat 6g,
Carbs (Fiber/Sugars) 19g (6g/11g),
Protein 4g

Sweet Pudding

Yields 5 cups

2 cups unsweetened coconut water

1¼ cups frozen peeled pineapple

¼ peeled avocado

2 cups fresh spinach

1 cup fresh zucchini

1 heaping scoop Nutiva hemp protein

Optional: 1 teaspoon grated fresh
   ginger

Nutrition per cup: 65 Calories, Fat 1g,
Carbs (Fiber/Sugars) 13g (2g/9g),
Protein 3g

Pine and Lime

Yields 4½–5 cups

1½ cups frozen peeled pineapple

2 cups fresh spinach

½ medium peeled avocado

½ peeled lime

⅓ cup fresh mint leaves

2 cups unsweetened coconut water

Optional: 1 teaspoon grated fresh
   ginger

Nutrition per cup: 85 Calories, Fat 3g,
Carbs (Fiber/Sugars) 16g (2g/12g),
Protein 1g

Berry Delicious

Yields 4 cups

1 cup strawberry

1 cup zucchini

1 cup frozen peeled mango

½ peeled lime

¼ cup fresh mint

2 cups unsweetened coconut water

Optional: 1 scoop Nutiva hemp
   protein

Nutrition per cup: 80 Calories, Fat 0g,
Carbs (Fiber/Sugars) 20g (3g/15g),
Protein 2g

Raspberry Mango and Me

Yields 3 cups

1 cup frozen peeled mango
½ cup frozen raspberries
1 tablespoon hemp seeds
1 pitted date
2 Persian cucumbers
1½ cups pure, unsweetened coconut water
Handful of fresh basil

Nutrition per cup: 120 Calories, Fat 2g, Carbs (Fiber/Sugars) 26g (4g/20g), Protein 2g

Skinny Cherry

Yields 4 cups

½ cup unfiltered water
1 cup unsweetened coconut water
½ cup fresh aloe vera gel
1 cup fresh spinach
1 cup frozen peeled pineapple
1 tablespoon ground flaxseed
1 cup pitted cherries
Juice from ½ fresh lemon
Handful of fresh mint

Nutrition per cup: 73 Calories, Fat 1g, Carbs (Fiber/Sugars) 15g (2g/11g), Protein 1g

Minty Limey Goodness

Yields 3½ cups

½ cup fresh aloe vera gel

1 cup frozen peeled mango

1 medium fresh pitted peach

1½ cups pure unsweetened coconut water

2 tablespoons fresh lime juice

1 scoop hemp protein

Handful of fresh mint leaves

Nutrition per cup: 90 Calories, Fat 1g, Carbs (Fiber/Sugars) 22g (4g/14g), Protein 4g

LOW SUGAR (<5 GRAMS OF SUGAR PER SERVING)

Guilt-Free Cinnamon Roll

Yields 3 cups

½ cup gluten-free oats soaked for at least 8 hours in 1 cup almond milk

½ cup water and few ice cubes

2 cups spinach

½ pitted date

Pinch of cinnamon

3–4 drops vanilla extract

Nutrition per cup: 99 Calories, Fat 2g, Carbs (Fiber/Sugars) 16g (4g/3g), Protein 3g

Purple Power

Yields 3 cups

4–5 coffee cubes

½ cup gluten-free oats soaked for at least 8 hours in 1 cup almond milk

½ cup almond milk (in addition to the almond milk that the oats were soaked in)

½ cup frozen blueberries

Pinch of cinnamon

1 tablespoon almond butter

Nutrition per cup: 128 Calories, Fat 5g, Carbs (Fiber/Sugars) 16g (3g/3g), Protein 4g

Thanksgiving in a Cup

Yields 3 cups

1 cup fresh spinach

1 cup unsweetened almond milk

1 small sweet potato, cooked

¼ teaspoon ground cinnamon

½ tablespoon Manitoba hemp seeds

1 pitted date

Optional: ¼ teaspoon ground nutmeg

Nutrition per cup: 85 Calories, Fat 2g, Carbs (Fiber/Sugars) 15g (3g/5g), Protein 2g

Salad Dressing

Yields 4 cups

½ yellow bell pepper
1 large Roma tomato
½ peeled avocado
½ peeled lime
1 cup packed fresh spinach
¼ teaspoon Himalayan salt
1½ cups water
¼ cup walnuts

Nutrition per cup: 97 Calories, Fat 8g,
Carbs (Fiber/Sugars) 6g (3g/2g), Protein 3g

Swiss Army Knife

Yields 4 cups

1 large pitted peach
2 stalks of Swiss chard, stems removed
½ medium peeled avocado
1 cup almond milk
½ cup water
1 pitted date
1 tablespoon hemp seeds

Nutrition per cup: 80 Calories, Fat 5g,
Carbs (Fiber/Sugars) 8g (3g/5g), Protein 2g

Pistachio Crush

Yields 4 cups

½ zucchini
1 medium pitted peach
2 cups fresh spinach
1 tablespoon pistachios
1 tablespoon hemp protein
1 teaspoon grated fresh ginger
1 teaspoon Matcha tea powder
1½ cups unsweetened almond milk

Nutrition per cup: 62 Calories, Fat 3g,
Carbs (Fiber/Sugars) 8g (3g/4g), Protein 3g

Two Peas in a Pod

Yields 2 cups

1 cup unsweetened almond milk

1 cup fresh spinach

1 tablespoon Almond & Macadamia
Nut Butter (page 58)

1 tablespoon hemp seeds

1 scoop Naked pea protein

Optional: Cacao nibs to sprinkle on
top

Nutrition per cup: 138 Calories, Fat 9g,
Carbs (Fiber/Sugars) 5g (2g/1g), Protein 11g

Almond Licious

Yields 2½ cups

1½ cups unsweetened almond milk

1 teaspoon matcha tea

1 tablespoon almond butter

1 scoop Nutiva hemp protein

½ peeled avocado

2 pinches cinnamon powder

Few ice cubes

Nutrition per cup: 148 Calories, Fat 11g,
Carbs (Fiber/Sugars) 8g (7g/1g), Protein 7g

The Deluxe

Yields 3 cups

⅓ cup gluten-free oats soaked for at
least 8 hours in 1 cup almond milk

½ cup unsweetened almond milk (in
addition to the almond milk used to
soak the oats)

1 tablespoon Almond & Macadamia
Nut Butter (page 58)

⅓ cup frozen raspberries

⅓ cup frozen blueberries

½ fresh medium-sized zucchini

2 pinches cinnamon powder

1 tablespoon ground flax powder

Optional: 1 scoop of your favorite
protein powder

Optional: Replace flax powder with
chia seeds

Nutrition per cup: 227 Calories, Fat 15g,
Carbs (Fiber/Sugars) 19g (7g/5g), Protein 6g

FARNOOSH'S FAVORITE SMOOTHIES

Figgy Sweet

Yields 6 cups

2 cup fresh spinach

½ bunch fresh parsley

4 stalks kale, stems removed

1 cup frozen pineapple

6 frozen small figs

1 cup frozen or fresh aloe vera gel

1 scoop hemp or other protein
   powder

¼ teaspoon spirulina

¼ teaspoon Himalayan salt

Juice of ½ lemon

2 cups filtered water

Nutrition per cup: 66 Calories, Fat 1g,
Carbs (Fiber/Sugars) 14g (3g/10g), Protein 3g

Happy Tummy

Yields 2 cups

1 cup unsweetened almond milk

1 teaspoon matcha

1 frozen peeled banana

1 tablespoon cashew butter

1 cup fresh spinach

Nutrition per cup: 127 Calories, Fat 6g,
Carbs (Fiber/Sugars) 18g (3g/8g), Protein 3g

Banana Split

Yields 4 cups

2 cups spinach

1½ tablespoons almond butter

1 frozen peeled banana

1 cup frozen blueberries

1 cup unsweetened almond milk

1–2 drops vanilla extract

1 cup filtered water

Nutrition per cup: 102 Calories, Fat 5g, Carbs (Fiber/Sugars) 15g (3g/8g), Protein 2g

Apple of My Eye

Yields 3 cups

2 cups fresh broccoli

2 small apples, core removed

Juice of ½ lemon

1 teaspoon matcha tea

1 tablespoon hemp seeds

¼ teaspoon spirulina

1½ cups water

1 tablespoon maple syrup

Nutrition per cup: 104 Calories, Fat 2g, Carbs (Fiber/Sugars) 21g (4g/15g), Protein 2g

Rawkstar Smoothie

Yields 5½ cups

½ raw beet

2 raw carrots

1 teaspoon grated fresh ginger

½ cup frozen blueberries

6 small frozen figs

1 tablespoon hemp hearts

¼ teaspoon coconut oil

¼ cup walnuts

2 cups water

Nutrition per cup: 120 Calories, Fat 5g, Carbs (Fiber/Sugars) 19g (4g/15g), Protein 3g

Berry Lucky

Yields 4 cups

½ açaí pack
½ cup blueberries
1½ cups cashew milk
1 frozen peeled banana
1 cup fresh spinach
1 tablespoon hemp seeds
¼ teaspoon coconut oil
1 teaspoon cacao powder
1 teaspoon raw honey
1 teaspoon spirulina

Nutrition per cup: 86 Calories, Fat 3g, Carbs (Fiber/Sugars) 14g (2g/9g), Protein 2g

Fortify Me Now

Yields 4 cups

1 cup fresh spinach
1 cup frozen or fresh aloe vera gel
1 cup unsweetened cashew milk
1½ cup filtered water
1 cup zucchini
1 scoop Nutiva hemp protein
1 tablespoon hemp hearts

½ teaspoon coconut oil
2 pitted dates
Dash of cinnamon
Optional: Fresh mint

Nutrition per cup: 74 Calories, Fat 2g, Carbs (Fiber/Sugars) 14g (3g/11g), Protein 3g

CHAPTER 6
HEALING COOL TONICS AND SHOTS

In this chapter, you learn how to make tonics and health shots using minimal equipment and in as little as two minutes—or however fast you can wash, mix, chop, slice, or grate a few ingredients! Some recipes require a bit of wait time while your ingredients marinate, but for most, you won't even need to get out your blender or juicer to whip up these delicious magic potions.

The way we define health tonics—sometimes also called immunity tonics or herbal tonics—is simple: concentrated caffeine-free, nutrient-rich drinks made

through the steeping of any combination of herbs, spices, select fruits, oils, vinegar, and vegetable roots. You consume these health tonics chilled and in quantities of one or two shots. You would usually want to accompany a shot with a small snack if your tonic is strong. I like to drink my tonic after a workout or yoga and follow with some water and maybe a few salty nuts.

Health tonics have tons of benefits. They can help reduce inflammation, improve digestion, calm the nervous system, act as an energizing boost, and enhance your immune system. Because the nutritional information of these tonics is nearly negligible as far as calories are concerned, we have not included that information in this section. But rest assured, they are packed with nutrition!

The quantity produced by all of these recipes is only slightly more than the liquid base you use. Some tonic recipes you'll find online or in other books ask that you let the drinks sit in a cold, dark cabinet for a month before they are ready to consume. We did not have the patience to wait that long, and we are guessing that you don't either. So the "marinating" time for the tonics in this book is between one to two hours. Please take note of steep time in each recipe and consume it within a week.

COOL TONICS

Sunshine Coconut, Ginger, and Turmeric Tonic

After making this delicious, refreshing, and zingy tonic, you might just be in heaven! The coconut water that I use religiously is C2O, as previously mentioned. Get an unsweetened coconut water with just coconut water as the ingredient, and with low sugar content, which indicates that the juice is from a young coconut. You'll be loving this tonic on hot summer days. It's also a perfect refreshing drink to serve friends by the pool or at a health-conscious party!

Ingredients

4 cups unsweetened coconut water

¼ cup fresh ginger slices

¼ cup fresh turmeric slices

2 teaspoons fresh lemongrass, finely chopped

8 cardamom pods, crushed

1 lime, thinly sliced

3–4 pinches cayenne pepper

Instructions

Add all ingredients into a glass jar with an airtight lid and place in the refrigerator. Set your timer for an hour, but don't let it steep for more than 75 minutes. I find that any more and it gets a little too spicy! After the timer goes off, strain your tonic into another container and either serve it with fresh mint or by itself, or place back in the fridge to consume at a later time. Be sure to keep it either in a mason jar with a tight lid or any other glass container that is airtight. You can keep it in the fridge for up to a week.

Refreshing Galangal Cider

Galangal root, also referred to as Siamese ginger or Thai ginger, has fabulous health potency, and while it looks and belongs to a similar family as ginger and turmeric and other similar roots, the taste is very distinct. I would describe it as bitter but also refreshing. You can find galangal in Asian grocery stores as well as some regular grocers. This root is better sliced than grated, and it makes a most hydrating tonic that wakes up all your senses. This tonic can be a wonderful refreshing drink any time of day.

Ingredients

20 grams galangal, thinly sliced

⅛ cup fresh mint

1 teaspoon fresh thyme

Zest of ½ blood orange (or other orange)

2 tablespoons raw, unfiltered apple cider vinegar

1 cinnamon stick, chopped into a few pieces

2 teaspoons raw honey dissolved first in 2 teaspoons hot water

2 cups filtered water

Optional: frozen 5–6 Tie Guan Yin Oolong tea cubes

Instructions

Add all ingredients into a glass jar with an airtight lid and place in the refrigerator. Set your timer for an hour, or at the most, 75 minutes. After the timer goes off, strain it all out into another container and either serve it or store back in the fridge to consume at a later time. Be sure to keep it either in a mason jar with a tight lid or any other glass container that is airtight. You can keep it in the fridge for up to a week.

You can also make oolong galangal iced tea. If you have Tie Guan Yin, which is a fabulous and common oolong tea, you can steep a cup of it, then pour it out into your ice cube tray. After it freezes, add your oolong ice cubes to the container with your Galangal Cider, and let it sit in the fridge for another hour. Serve cold and enjoy!

Spicy Pomegranate and Coconut Tonic

This delicious, rejuvenating, and stimulating tonic has it all. There's a touch of sourness from pomegranate, the aroma from basil and oregano, a kick from the spicy jalapeño and ginger . . . and when they mix with the coconut water, it delivers the perfect tonic.

Ingredients

⅓ cup pomegranate seeds, crushed

½ fresh jalapeño pepper, seeded and minced

⅛ cup ginger slices

⅓ to ½ lemon, sliced

⅛ cup fresh oregano and mint leaves

2 cups unsweetened coconut water

Instructions

Add all ingredients into your glass jar and let it steep in the fridge for 1 hour. Set your timer for an hour, or at most, 75 minutes. After the timer goes off, strain it all out into another container and either serve it or place back in the fridge to consume at a later time. Be sure to keep it either in a mason jar with a tight lid or any other glass container that is airtight. You can keep it in the fridge for up to a week.

Cooling Peppermint Herb Tonic

Lemongrass, which is mainly used in Thai cooking, has a most energizing scent. It makes a fabulous tonic in this recipe along with fresh herbs, orange slices, turmeric, apple cider vinegar, and a touch of peppermint.

Ingredients

2 cups filtered water

1 tablespoon fresh thyme, crushed

⅛ cup chopped fresh dill, crushed

⅛ cup turmeric, thinly sliced

⅛ cup chopped cilantro, crushed

⅛ cup lemongrass, chopped

½ orange, thinly sliced

7–8 drops peppermint oil

1 tablespoon pure maple syrup

Instructions

Slice up the unpeeled orange. Add all ingredients into your glass container. Steep it in the fridge for an hour, or at the most, 75 minutes. After the timer goes off, strain it all out into another container and either serve it or place back in the fridge to consume at a later time. Be sure to keep it either in a mason jar with a tight lid or any other glass container that is airtight. You can keep it in the fridge for up to a week.

Golden Yellow Spicy Garlic Tonic

This tonic requires a little more prep time as you'll need your juicer to juice the orange and a lemon, but the extra effort is totally worth it. Think of it as a juice and tonic fusion with spicy garlic and ginger. The citrus flavor of fresh-squeezed juice and the amazing benefits of apple cider vinegar will deliver loads of goodies to your body. This is one of my favorites!

Ingredients

Fresh juice of 1 peeled
    orange
Fresh juice of 1 lemon
1 cup filtered water
2 tablespoons raw honey
3 cloves garlic, pressed
2 tablespoons thinly sliced
    or grated ginger
1 cinnamon stick, crushed
⅛ cup raw, unfiltered
    apple cider vinegar

Instructions

Add all ingredients into your glass container. Steep it in the fridge for an hour, or at the most, 75 minutes. After the timer goes off, strain it all out into another container and either serve it or place back in the fridge to consume at a later time. Be sure to keep it either in a mason jar with a tight lid or any other glass container that is airtight. You can keep it in the fridge for up to a week.

Berry Good Hydrating Tonic

For hot summer days, make yourself this delicious healing tonic with fresh berries, ginger, sage, and cucumber. It will help you cool down, hydrate, and consume some healing nutrients.

Ingredients

½ cup blueberries, crushed

4 strawberries, crushed

1 tablespoon minced ginger

5 leaves of sage, stems removed, crushed

20 Thai basil leaves, crushed

1 Persian cucumber, diced

4 cups filtered water

Optional: 1 tablespoon raw honey dissolved in 1 tablespoon hot water

Optional: 2 slices of lime

Instructions

Add all ingredients to a glass jar and refrigerate for one hour. Strain. The berries soak up a lot of water, even if they were crushed, so gently press on the strainer to release all the juice. If the tonic too strong, add a little honey. This tonic tastes best chilled, so feel free to add ice cubes. You can keep it in the fridge for up to a week.

Farnoosh's Magic Potion Tonic Recipe

My dad has been going on and on about the benefits of apple cider vinegar (ACV) for as long as I can remember. When my brother's new mother-in-law started talking about her habit of taking ACV religiously as a preventative measure against general onset of illness, I started to get more curious about it. It turns out ACV is the most popular type of vinegar in the natural health community and is claimed to have enormous health benefits, some of which are well proven by science. You may hear of "ACV with the mother," which is the same as raw, unfiltered ACV and simply refers to the strands of proteins and enzymes and healthy bacteria that show up in unfiltered apple cider. That's what gives it the slightly murky appearance when you shake the bottle. You want this kind of raw, unfiltered ACV for maximum health benefits.

With this recipe, in addition to our raw, unfiltered ACV, I decided to throw in a few other highly potent ingredients such as garlic, ginger, turmeric, cayenne pepper, raw honey, and lemons. Below you'll find the preparation instructions to make what I call my Magic Potion Tonic Recipe as well as suggestions on how and when to consume it.

Ingredients for Phase 1

9–10 cloves garlic, peeled

3 unpeeled lemons

1–1½ cups fresh ginger root

¾–1 cup fresh turmeric root

Note: If you can't find fresh turmeric root, you can substitute with 1 tablespoon turmeric powder dissolved in 1 tablespoon of hot water. You can do the same with ground ginger rather than fresh ginger root. I do recommend going for the fresh roots of both if at all possible.

Instructions for Phase 1

Juice everything in your juicer. It's best to use a masticating slow juicer that completely juices the ingredients.

Next, you'll need the following ingredients:

Ingredients for Phase 2

2 tablespoons raw honey

1–1¼ cups raw, unfiltered apple cider vinegar

1 teaspoon cayenne pepper

Optional: 3–4 drops rosemary essential oil

Instructions for Phase 2

Dissolve your honey in 2 tablespoons of hot water. Then add that and remaining Phase 2 ingredients into your juice made in Phase 1. Stir everything for one minute. Store in an airtight glass container for up to two weeks in the refrigerator.

Take 1–2 tablespoons of your magic potion daily on an empty stomach and without diluting it. Immediately after, drink 16–24 oz. of filtered water. Then eat your breakfast. Be sure to eat within 15–20 minutes of drinking the potion, or you may feel nauseous. If you're not ready for a full meal just yet, have a few salty nuts with some water.

SPICY WAKE-ME-UP AND SOOTHING NIGHTCAP SHOTS

Anti-Inflammatory Spicy Wake-Me-Up Shot

This cold, latte-like drink can be whipped up in two minutes. It is perfect for mornings when you don't have a lot of time. You most likely already have turmeric powder, cayenne pepper, and ginger powder in your spice cabinet. I love this wake-me-up for the anti-inflammatory benefits of the spices. Plus, it's delicious! I've found that these spice powders dissolve best in hot water, but you don't want to raise the temperature of your cold milk either, so use no more than two tablespoons to dissolve the powders, let it sit for a minute to cool slightly, then add your cold nut milk. This is a spicy drink with a warming after-effect. It will help your muscles release inflammation and it can also be great for any digestion issues or act as a quick detox before the start of your day.

Ingredients

- ½ teaspoon turmeric powder
- ¼ teaspoon ginger powder
- ⅛ teaspoon cayenne pepper
- ½ cup almond or cashew milk

Instructions

Dissolve all ingredients in 1–2 tablespoons of hot water. Allow to cool for 1 minute. Add cold almond or cashew milk. Mix and drink it up.

Trace Minerals Nightcap Shot

Do you get your trace minerals? Our bodies need tiny amounts of minerals such as iron, zinc, selenium, fluoride, chromium, copper, iodine, and magnesium on a daily basis. A versatile and healthy diet can and often does contain most of these minerals, but then again, how often do we have days when life happens and we can't prioritize complete, healthy meals? While getting your trace minerals from a natural food source is the best option, what's most important is that you get them one way or another on a daily basis. Supplements are one way to get them, but my preferred method is in powder form so that your body can absorb it as quickly and efficiently as possible.

For the past three years, I've kept a bottle of Mezotrace in my cupboard, and every night, before bed, I make my soothing pre-sleep nightcap. What I love about Mezotrace is that it tastes delicious when mixed with just a little nut milk. While taste buds can vary, I can say that my neighbor agrees, too. She not only loves it, but after taking this for a week, her splitting headaches disappeared. I'm not promising that Mezotrace is a cure-all, but if you're low on your trace minerals, this can be a quick fix and an easy, healing drink to incorporate into your daily habits. You don't have to stick with Mezotrace brand either. You can search other brands that offer these essential minerals in powdered form for your healing nightcap!

Ingredients

½ teaspoon Mezotrace
   or your choice of
   powdered minerals
½ cup almond or cashew
   milk, or even water

Instructions

Mix until powder is dissolved, and drink.

CHAPTER 7

HOT ELIXIRS, DELICIOUS TEAS, AND CREAMY NON-DAIRY LATTES

We've gone from juices to smoothies to healing tonics and now have arrived at healing elixirs. Elixirs are hot drinks made with herbs, spices, superfoods, and other healing nutrients. Elixirs are liquid refreshments to nourish your body and mind on multiple levels. With all the nutrients and vitamins and minerals, these warm beverages can be therapeutic, even medicinal, and highly beneficial to your overall health and well-being.

The elixirs in this book do not require the use of juicers or blenders, except for the latte elixirs. You can prepare most of the ingredients for your elixirs simply by chopping, grating, or crushing them. The bases of our elixirs are either hot water or a type of tea. Elixirs generally are less dense than your smoothies, use herbs and spices, have little to no fruit and no leafy greens, and are served hot or warm. You steep or boil your elixir ingredients and then strain to serve. You can often steep your elixir mix for a second time.

Elixirs can be great first thing in the morning, before or after you take in your first batch of filtered water, but they can be enjoyed any time. Beware of the few caffeine-containing elixirs during the evening hours if caffeine interferes with your sleep.

This chapter is divided into four parts. We start off with the most therapeutic and healing teas, followed by non-caffeine hot elixirs. Then we have what I call "tea elixirs," which are healing drinks containing low to medium amounts of caffeine, depending on the type of tea used, and additional healing ingredients. Last but not least, we have the non-dairy superfood latte elixirs. These are foamy on top just like a latte, but without dairy products. Only one of the lattes contains a little caffeine, due to the matcha tea in it.

Now that you have an idea about the world of elixirs, let's dive in and make your first one!

A Peaceful World Is Run on Loose-Leaf Premium Quality Tea

I cannot over-emphasize the importance of your tea quality and its source. We live in a world of tea bags and lukewarm water passed up as "tea." No wonder coffee is more popular! Most tea bags are whatever is left over from broken tea leaves, also known as the "dust and fannings." Higher quality loose-leaf teas use

the full leaf and have more essential oils, aroma, and release the right amount of tannins when properly brewed with the right temperature water. Loose-leaf tea has more nutritional potency and creates the best flavor and the most authentic tea experience. Tea bags compromise tea's health benefits, aroma, taste, and overall experience of what tea is meant to be. When tea bags are steeped, they often result in bitter, astringent brews because of their lower quality. So for that and other reasons, I recommend that you only ever using high-end loose-leaf tea if you want the full benefits and best flavor from your tea.

Now, I am not saying that all tea bags are created equal, nor do I claim that all loose-leaf tea is top quality. Some tea brands produce relatively high-quality tea bags, and if you look carefully, you can see larger tea leaves inside the tea bag as compared to just the "dust and fanning" in most thin, square tea bags.

Loose-leaf tea is sold in bulk in specialty stores, although some health grocery stores carry it in their tea section. Store it in an airtight container at room temperature at home. As with everything, when you are going up in grade and quality, you will also see an increase in price, but think of it as investment in your health.

You need a few accessories to properly prepare and brew your loose-leaf tea. As we mentioned in the Hot Water Therapy section, a water boiler appliance such as the Zojirushi in your kitchen can be a wonderful way to prepare your hot beverages. Otherwise, you can use a kettle and bring your filtered water to boil every time you want to drink tea. You will need a teapot, a strainer, as well as proper clear tea glasses. Never pour tea in a mug used for coffee or other drinks. As convenient as they may seem, I also find that travel stainless steel travel mugs alter the taste of tea ever so slightly. If possible, use glass tumblers

for when you are on the go. Use a clear glass or ceramic one specifically designed for tea.

Below you will find my top recommended teas that not only promote general health, but also taste delicious and might just move you away from a coffee addiction, if you have one.

Oolong Tea: Heavenly Milk Oolong

If you've never tasted milk oolong tea, I'm excited for you to experience this delicious, creamy tea. Fear not, there is no actual milk here. The word "milk" refers to the creaminess of this special oolong tea, also known as Guangzhou tea, which is a Chinese tea full of antioxidants and health benefits that are out of this world. It is a miracle drink for easing digestion and helping with elimination.

This tea is darker than your green teas and lighter than your black teas. If you can, shop for your milk oolong in person (rather than online) and do a smell test; have them shake the container and smell it for an unmistakably delicious aroma. If you don't smell anything, it's not as fresh or it may be regular oolong rather than milk oolong. Since this tea is quite expensive, make sure to follow the instructions below to get the most out of every single ounce!

Over the past fifteen years, I've experimented with a lot of milk oolong teas. Some of my favorite brands are The Republic of Tea (online), David's Tea (Canada or online), and TeaMalchi (online).

Milk oolong has a golden yellow color with beautiful leaves that unfurl as they steep. You can re-steep it once or even twice. Use the same instructions as below and re-steep for 5–6 minutes. I let it go slightly longer on the second steep. You can experiment with a third steep and see if it gets too weak.

If you won't be re-steeping the same day, discard the leaves. If you are determined to reuse your tea leaves the next day, dry them with a paper towel after you're done steeping for the first day, and keep them in a dry container to avoid bacterial growth.

I recommend you try this tea first without any raw honey or maple syrup and then decide if you want to add a little sweetness.

Ingredients

1 tablespoon milk oolong
tea

1½ cups hot water,
just below boiling
temperature (200–205°F)

Instructions

Always use filtered water; tap water is too flat and can affect the taste of your delicious oolong. Oolong tea leaves are more delicate than black tea leaves, and so be careful not to burn them. Your hot water should be below boiling temperature. Bring your water to boil on the stove and then let it cool for 30 seconds, or alternatively use your water boiler. Then pour it over your tea leaves. Steep for 4–5 minutes. Serve and enjoy!

Oolong Tea: Tie Guan Yin and Raw Honey

I fell in love with the meaning of Tie Guan Yin (also spelled Tie Kuan Yin some places) before the taste. The name translates to Iron Goddess of Mercy, and it lives up to its name every bit. This Chinese traditional tea is a premium loose-leaf tea with loads of health benefits. When I had first quit coffee, this was my go-to healing drink. It did wonders for my digestion and nerves and helped me lose weight.

Similar to milk oolong, this tea also re-steeps well. Follow the same instructions on re-steeping and usage of tea leaves as milk oolong (page 135).

Ingredients

1 tablespoon Tie Guan Yin

1 teaspoon raw honey

1½ cups hot water,
just below boiling
temperature (200–205°F)

Instructions

Always use filtered water; tap water is too flat and can affect the taste of your delicious Oolong. Oolong tea leaves are more delicate than black tea leaves, so be careful not to burn them. Your hot water for this tea should be below boiling temperature. Bring your water to boil on the stove and then let it cool for 30 seconds, or alternatively use your water boiler. Then pour it over your tea leaves. Steep for 4–5 minutes. Serve and enjoy!

Black Tea: Cream of Earl Grey

The queen of all black teas is Cream of Earl Grey. Earl Grey tea, as you know, offers more aroma and less bitterness than English breakfast tea, thanks to a delicious citrus fruit called bergamot. In order to make Earl Grey tea, they take the leaves from the Camellia sinensis plant, a tea plant, and combine it with bergamot oil, the essence extracted from the fruit's skin. Now to make Cream of Earl Grey, they go one step further and throw in dried blue cornflowers, and sometimes a hint of vanilla, and voilà, you have the most perfect tea to wake you from your sweet slumber and perk you up for your day.

In exploring many brands of Cream of Earl Grey, my favorites boil down to Plum Deluxe's Mindful Morning, Sloane Tea (Canada), Fortnum & Mason (England), Tealyra (online), David's Tea (Canada or online), and Tea Thyme's Earl Grey Supreme (Orangeburg, SC), all of which make divinely delicious blends.

Ingredients

1 tablespoon Cream of Earl Grey

1½ cups boiling hot water (212°F)

Instructions

Pour the boiling hot water over the tea leaves in your teapot and let steep for 5 minutes. Strain and enjoy. I recommend using glass or porcelain for black tea so you can see the color. You can discard or re-steep. I like to re-steep my Earl Grey by adding an additional teaspoon and steeping for 6 minutes. After the second round, discard and start fresh.

Green Teas: Dragonwell and Sencha

With the popularity of green tea in the western world, no doubt you've tried it at least once. What did you think? First time you try it, green tea may taste bitter and unappealing. It is definitely a more acquired taste, and as your taste buds adjust to less sugary drinks, you may come to appreciate this green cup of goodness, claimed by some as the "healthiest beverage on the planet!" Green tea leaves go through less withering and oxidation than their oolong and black tea counterparts. To get the maximum benefits of green tea, trade your tea bags for the high-quality loose-leaf kind.

There is a world of green teas out there. When you walk the Depachikas, the underground massive food department stores in Tokyo found at the bottom of most shopping centers, the aisles of green tea can make you dizzy. It's fun to experiment with different kinds, and after years of doing so, I have selected my two favorites: Dragonwell or Longjing, which is a Chinese tea, and sencha, which is a Japanese tea. Sencha is a Japanese green tea and quite common in Japan. It is made through a process of steaming and rolling the leaves. Dragonwell is a Chinese green tea with long flat leaves and a beautiful aroma. This tea is pan roasted from the area of Longjing Village in China. This is one of China's most famous green teas and it is delicious, with a signature chestnut aroma that leaves you swooning.

For a third and fourth recommendation, I'd add gyokuro and matcha teas and my husband's vote would go to hojicha, which is a roasted green tea. Gyokuro, matcha, and hojicha are also Japanese teas.

You can find high-quality loose-leaf tea online or in specialty tea shops. I also love Abundance Blend Green Tea by Plum Deluxe, which has sencha green tea plus elderflowers, calendula, and passion fruit extract. Absolutely divine. It even re-steeps beautifully for a second time.

Ingredients

1 teaspoon of your
favorite green tea
1 cup (8 oz) hot water
(185–195°F)

Instructions

With green tea, it is especially important not to burn your leaves and not to steep them too long as the tea will get bitter. You want just the right balance with water temperature and steep time. Warm your glass by pouring some hot water in it and letting it sit while you steep your tea. Add your tea leaves to your teapot, then pour in the hot water. Brew for 2–3 minutes only. You can also get additional infusions from Dragonwell and sencha teas. Increase your brew time by 30 seconds to 1 minute each time you re-steep your leaves and repeat up to three times. Enjoy!

White Teas: Silver Needle and White Peony

For the longest time, I could not appreciate white tea. I much preferred the stronger flavored teas. Still, keeping an open mind helped me fall in love with the right white tea! White tea is the least processed of the three teas (green, black, white) and thus it retains a high amount of antioxidants, and with its lower caffeine dosage, you can consume it later in the day without fear of insomnia.

White tea is the young or minimally processed leaves of the Camellia sinensis plant. Your most common white teas are the silver needle (BaiHaoYinzhen) and the white peony (BaiMudan or PaiMuTan). White tea makes a mild tea and has a lovely calming effect. You can often find these teas blended with dried fruit such as peach, apricot, or pomegranate, or some other berry, as well as herbs such as hibiscus. Plum Deluxe makes a delicious white tea with peaches, apricots, marigold petals, and pear essence, and Republic of Tea has delicious premium PaiMuTan loose-leaf tea. Yum!

Ingredients

1 teaspoon of your
   favorite white tea
1½ cups hot water
   (185–195°F)

Instructions

Just as with green tea, take care not to burn your leaves. Your water should be well below the boiling point. White tea steeps in 4–5 minutes, or you can let it go longer if you have a blended tea as they normally do not get bitter with longer steeping. Enjoy!

GABA Tea

GABA (or gamma-aminobutyric acid) is a necessary neurotransmitter that our nervous system uses, specifically for the regulation of muscle tone. GABA tea, first created by Dr. Tsushida Tojiro of Japan, is a tea that has undergone a special oxygen-free fermentation process, and as a result has accumulated GABA in the leaves. We became familiar with GABA tea thanks to TeaMalchi who was kind enough to send us multiple samples to taste. They have dozens of GABA teas of the highest quality, so you are bound to find a flavor that satisfies your taste buds.

Follow the preparation instructions for milk oolong (page 135) to prepare and re-steep this tea for extra infusions. You can use raw honey to sweeten it if desired. Some of our top picks from TeaMalchi were:

1. TeaMalchi Sapphire GABA Oolong. The medium roast has a delicious and beautiful golden color with a rich earthy taste. Helps you to get to sleep faster and aids weight loss.
2. TeaMalchi Ruby GABA Oolong. The heavy roast is a ruby dark tea with a crisp, mellow, nutty taste and a lovely fragrance. The light roast is a light yellow tea that helps with digestion and mental strength.
3. TeaMalchi Turquoise GABA Green Tea. The light roast is very light in caffeine and helps with hypertension and blood pressure.
4. TeaMalchi Diamond GABA Oolong. The medium roast has a light, flowery, and sweet aroma. This flavorful oolong is great for detoxification, assisting with hypertension as well as collagen production.

DELICIOUS HOT HERBAL AND SPICE ELIXIRS

Hot elixirs are so much fun to make. These elixirs are completely free of caffeine. The ingredients primarily come from herbs and spices. To make the perfectly delicious and aroma-inducing mouth-watering elixirs here, here are some easy guidelines to follow:

1. As much as possible, either grow your own herbs or buy them fresh. The powder or dried form of the herbs will do in a pinch, but to get the full benefits and the best aroma and flavors, go fresh.
2. Always use filtered tap water for your hot water.
3. Use a proper teapot made of either ceramic or glass and one that is exclusively used for tea, never for coffee or other drinks.
4. Serve your hot elixirs in a heat-resistant glass, not a mug or a plastic cup.
5. Never use the microwave to warm up an elixir that has cooled down. Heat it over the stove.

Now you are ready to get started. Remember, these elixirs will be doing your body so much good, and they will taste delicious to boot!

Lemongrass Ginger Thyme Elixir

This homemade herbal hot drink is easy to make, and all the ingredients can easily be found in your local grocery store. It is also packed with nutrients that your body will love. If you like to grow your own herbs, you can put them to good use with this recipe. This is a lovely after-dinner drink to help with digestion and doesn't contain any caffeine. It re-steeps well at least once. It is virtually impossible for any packaged herbal tea bag to taste this fresh! After making your homemade herbal drinks with fresh ingredients, I bet you'll never go back to herbal tea bags.

Yields 1 serving

Ingredients

1 tablespoon fresh mint
1 teaspoon fresh
    lemongrass
1 teaspoon fresh thyme
½ teaspoon grated ginger
¼ teaspoon fennel seeds
1–1¼ cups boiling water
Optional: ½ teaspoon raw
    honey, or to taste

Instructions

Crush your herbs in a mortar and pestle for extra flavor. Put all your ingredients in your teapot, then pour the hot water over it and steep 5–6 minutes. This tea re-steeps really nicely for a second time; leave it on for 7–8 minutes for a strong flavor.

Starstruck Multi-Herb Elixir

This homemade herbal tea is slightly sweetened with honey, cinnamon, and star anise. You can find this star-shaped, one-of-a-kind spice in regular grocery stores or order it online. The flavor of this tea is three-fold: herbal, sweet, and spicy, and it is perfect for an afternoon of relaxation, reading, or contemplating.

Yields 2 servings

Ingredients

1 teaspoon fresh rosemary

1 teaspoon fresh thyme

½ teaspoon fresh oregano

1 teaspoon fresh basil

1 star anise

Zest of ½ medium orange

1 cinnamon stick

1 teaspoon raw honey

2½ cups hot water (195–205°F)

Instructions

Crush your herbs in a mortar and pestle for extra flavor. Add herbs and other ingredients to the teapot, then pour the hot water over it and steep for 5–6 minutes. If you prefer a stronger flavor, you can skip the honey or use only two cups of hot water. This tea also re-steeps nicely for a second time; leave it on for 7–8 minutes for a strong flavor.

Lavender and Orange Zest Dream Elixir

This delicious lavender tea is a wonderful healing and calming nightcap. Lavender is known for reducing anxiety, calming emotional stress, and improving sleep. You can buy dried lavender at most grocery stories, and as long as you stock fennel seeds and the occasional orange, you can make this tea regularly. This is the perfect hot drink before bed, with just a touch of sweetness from pure maple syrup infused with the citrus flavor from your orange.

Yields 1 serving

Ingredients

1 teaspoon pure maple syrup

1 tablespoon fennel seeds

1 teaspoon lavender

Zest of ½ medium orange

1½ cups hot water (195–205°F)

Instructions

Add all ingredients to teapot and steep for 5 minutes. You can re-steep this tea a second time for 7–8 minutes.

Herbal Apple Cider and Honey Elixir

Apple cider vinegar and honey are made for each other. Curious what happens when you add herbs to the mixture? This hot herbal elixir is delicious and full of healing powers for better digestion. It also helps to relieve a sore throat and has been said by many to aid weight loss to boot.

Yields 2 servings

Ingredients

⅛ cup fresh rosemary

¼ cup fresh mint

⅛ cup fresh thyme

⅛ cup fresh lemongrass

1 tablespoon raw honey

2 tablespoons raw, unfiltered apple cider vinegar

2 cups hot water (195–205°F)

Instructions

Chop your fresh herbs into small pieces or, if you wish, crush them with your mortar and pestle. Then add them and all the other ingredients to your teapot. Steep 5–7 minutes, then strain. You can also add a touch of fresh lemon juice to your tea. Enjoy!

DELICIOUS HOT TEA ELIXIRS

These elixirs combine tea leaves with herbs and/or spices, so they do contain some caffeine. The tea elixirs give you a rejuvenating boost.

Earl Pomegranate Tea

Pomegranates are a divine fruit that symbolizes fertility and prosperity. They're low in sugar, high in nutritional content, beautiful to display, and available in most grocery stores. You can buy the pomegranate seeds, already cut and ready for use, or you can get the pomegranate itself. There is an easy trick to peeling and extracting pomegranate seeds: fill a bowl with cool water, cut the fruit in half, hold each half under water one at a time, and extract the seeds.

Earl Grey tea is very common; I would use loose-leaf Earl Grey from a high-quality brand. Earl Grey can come in different types such as cream of Earl Grey or regular Earl Grey. For this recipe, I would use regular straight-up Earl Grey without any cornflowers, vanilla, lavender, or other additives. My absolute favorite brands are Sloane Tea or David's Tea, both from Canada, Nina's Tea from Paris, Fortnum & Mason from England, and Tea Thyme of Orangeburg, SC. Or you can explore and find your favorite tea supplier!

This Earl Pomegranate Tea is inspired by my Iranian heritage, and it makes a most delicious morning beverage. It wakes up your senses with the aroma of cloves, the sweetness of pure maple syrup, and the tartness of the pomegranate.

Ingredients

1 tablespoon fresh
   pomegranate seeds
1 sprig fresh rosemary
¼ teaspoon cloves
1 tablespoon Earl Grey tea
1 teaspoon pure maple
   syrup
1½ cups boiling water

Instructions

Crush the pomegranate seeds and put them into your teapot. Strip the rosemary leaves off of the stem and add them in and then add the remaining ingredients. Pour your boiling water over the mixture and steep for 5 minutes. Strain into your favorite tea glass and enjoy. You may re-steep this a second time, although it may be weaker. Plain Earl Grey does not re-steep as well as green or oolong teas. If you really want to get a second cup and have it be the same strength as before, you can add an extra teaspoon of Earl Grey to the mix and re-steep.

If you like your tea nice and strong, you can use less maple syrup or skip it altogether.

Mint and Thyme Pomegranate Tea

This recipe makes for a perfect morning or early afternoon tea as it has caffeine in it from the black tea. You can use your favorite loose-leaf black tea for this recipe.

Yields 2 servings

Ingredients

2 tablespoons fresh pomegranate seeds

1 teaspoon lavender

1 tablespoon of your favorite loose-leaf black tea

1 teaspoon crushed fresh mint

1 teaspoon crushed fresh thyme

1 teaspoon raw honey

2½ cups boiling water

Instructions

Crush the pomegranate seeds and put them into your teapot. Add your fresh mint, fresh thyme, raw honey, and lavender and tea. Pour your boiling water over the mixture and steep for 5–6 minutes. Strain into your favorite tea glass and enjoy. You may re-steep this a second time, but it will be much weaker.

Barberry Orange Zest Black Tea

Barberry is a teeny tiny tart red berry often used in Persian cooking, especially with white basmati rice. We call it "zereshk" in Farsi. Barberry is packed with nutrients, and you can find this berry in dried fruit form in any Persian or Middle Eastern grocer. If you can't find barberry, you can use dried cranberry instead. In this two-part recipe, you'll be making a hot barberry tea with cloves, orange zest, and raw honey.

Ingredients for Part 1:

2 tablespoons dried
    barberry
¼ teaspoon cloves
Zest of ½ medium orange
1 tablespoon raw honey
1 cup boiling water
2–3 thin orange slices
Optional: Fresh mint

Ingredients for Part 2:

1 tablespoon loose-leaf
    black tea
1 cup boiling water

Instructions for Part 1:

Put all the ingredients above, except the orange slices, in a teapot and add 2 cups of boiling water over it. Steep for 15 minutes. When it's done, add the orange slices into the mix.

Instructions for Part 2:

As your barberry mix is steeping, prepare your favorite black tea. Pour your tea and hot water in your teapot. Steep for five minutes.

Mix the barberry tea with the black tea in equal parts. You may want to try the Part 1 of this recipe by itself and see if you like the taste without any tea. You may even cool it and drink it cold. Or you can enjoy it with the black tea as I do! Either way, you'll be getting your barberry boost! This recipe makes two servings.

Lavender & Cardamom Black Tea

This blend of black tea combines the wonderfully complex flavor of cardamom—spicy, herbal, citrusy, and fragrant—with an all-popular vanilla flavor and the soothing aroma and taste of lavender. You can use any loose-leaf high-grade plain black tea such as Ceylon or Assam in this recipe. It's a perfect tea for an afternoon of work, study, reading, or contemplation.

Yields 1 serving

Ingredients

1 teaspoon black tea

⅛ teaspoon lavender

4 crushed cardamom pods

4 drops vanilla extract

1½ cups boiling water

Zest of ⅓ lemon

Optional: 1 teaspoon
  maple syrup

Instructions

Add all the ingredients to your teapot and add the hot water last. Steep for five minutes. Pour and enjoy. I prefer this tea without the syrup, but you may like a little additional sweetness.

SUPERFOOD LATTES

I remember my real latte phase when I was living on espresso to stay "alert" in my corporate job. I would ignore my stomachaches, which were undoubtedly from too much strong caffeine combined with lactose from the milk. It eventually became clear that I had to give up the regular latte for many health reasons, but I still loved the texture and feel of a creamy, foamy warm beverage. Why give it up? While a typical standard latte from Starbucks is as far as you can get from healing, there is such a thing as a healthy latte.

In this section, I share five delicious, creamy, easy-to-make, dairy-free and, caffeine-free (with the exception of the matcha latte) latte recipes. I call them "superfood lattes" for fun. These lattes will leave you feeling good inside and out.

If you're not in the habit of making your own lattes, they may seem a bit of a "hassle" at first. I know I thought of it that way for a while, but let me just say, get

over it and go for it. Once I got over the little bit of preparation using the blender and the stove, I was making these creamy, silky, delicious, heart-warming and healing lattes with such ease. And I have to say, these lattes keep me satisfied for an hour or two. So let us make a healing latte, shall we?

Spicy Chai Latte

When you're feeling a little under the weather, slightly fatigued, or are experiencing body aches or chills from the seasons changing, this latte will give you the boost you need. The spices will warm you up, the sweetness will delight you, and the creaminess will match that of the best latte you've ever had! If you're sensitive to spices, use less cayenne pepper and ginger or dilute them with ¼ to ½ cup filtered water first.

Ingredients

⅛ teaspoon cinnamon or ½ cinnamon stick

⅛ teaspoon powdered ginger

6 crushed cloves

⅛ teaspoon vanilla extract

½ teaspoon crushed cardamom

1–2 pinches cayenne pepper

1 teaspoon maple syrup

1 cup cashew milk

Optional: ½ teaspoon star anise

Instructions

Blend everything in a high speed blender for one minute. Pour into a small saucepan. Heat until it just starts to simmer. Stop right before it comes to boil. Pour into your favorite latte mug, and enjoy.

Christina's Turmeric & Ginger Latte

Christina Canters is one of my star clients. She took my Business Apprenticeship program in 2017 and as part of her program, we went to Melbourne, Australia, for her in-person intensives. We both value health and well-being as entrepreneurs, and in our conversations, she shared this delicious latte that she often makes for breakfast. She raved about the benefits of drinking this latte all winter long and how good she felt. This is the only featured recipe by someone else in this book. It is spicy, filling, warm and cozy, sweet enough, and plenty satisfying, with the perfect spice kick for starting off the day with alertness and enthusiasm.

Ingredients

⅔ cup filtered water

⅔ cup unsweetened almond milk

¼ teaspoon grated fresh or powdered turmeric

¼ teaspoon grated fresh or powdered ginger

¼ teaspoon cinnamon

1 teaspoon coconut oil

1 teaspoon almond butter

1 teaspoon Manitoba Harvest hemp seeds

Optional: 1 teaspoon raw honey to taste

Instructions

Blend everything in a high speed blender for 1 minute. Pour into a small saucepan. Heat until it just starts to simmer. Stop right before it comes to boil. Pour into your favorite latte mug, sprinkle with more cinnamon, and enjoy!

Flat White Matcha Latte

This lovely cup of comforting, grounding, yet invigorating matcha latte is just what the doctor ordered. I like my matcha latte strong and so I use a full teaspoon of matcha, but my husband likes it less strong. Start with ½ teaspoon of matcha tea powder and adjust to your taste buds. This is a beautiful, delicious, as well as super quick and simple latte to wake up to! I love Full Leaf Tea or Republic of Tea's fine high-quality matcha tea selections.

Ingredients

½–1 teaspoon matcha tea powder

⅛ teaspoon coconut oil

1 teaspoon maple syrup

1 cup unsweetened almond milk

Instructions

Blend everything in a high speed blender for 1 minute. Pour into a small saucepan. Heat until it just starts to simmer. Stop right before it comes to a boil. Pour into your favorite latte mug, sprinkle coconut shreds on top if you like, and enjoy.

Silky Chocolate Coconut Latte

Who doesn't love hot chocolate? Even growing up in Iran, hot chocolate was a special treat that still brings back sweet memories. Here is a healthier, guilt-free version. This silky chocolate coconut latte is healthy, with a nice dose of good-for-you protein and fat, but be sure to make it with coconut milk. Almond milk and cashew milk may not give you the right consistency here. I used a can of coconut milk from Trader Joe's and even though it was "reduced fat," it made a really creamy latte.

Ingredients

¼ cup coconut milk

¾ cup filtered water

1 teaspoon maple syrup

1 teaspoon cacao powder

1 teaspoon almond butter

1 teaspoon hemp protein powder by Nutiva

1 teaspoon ground flaxseed

Instructions

Blend everything in a high speed blender for 1 minute. Pour into a small saucepan. Heat until it just starts to simmer. Stop right before it comes to boil. Pour into your favorite latte mug, sprinkle cacao nibs on top, and let them melt a little before taking your first sip.

Golden Latte with Apple and Lavender

For our last but not least latte recipe, I have combined some of my favorite ingredients into a delicious golden latte to soothe and comfort you during a lazy afternoon, or keep you company as you work away toward your goals and deadlines.

Ingredients

½ fresh apple

3–4 walnut halves

½ teaspoon cinnamon powder

1 teaspoon raw honey

½ teaspoon turmeric powder

½ teaspoon dried lavender

1 cup unsweetened almond milk

Optional: ⅛ teaspoon nutmeg

Instructions

Blend everything in a high speed blender for 1 minute. Pour into a small saucepan and throw in a cinnamon stick if you want more cinnamon taste. Heat until it just starts to simmer. Stop right before it comes to boil. Pour into your favorite latte mug, and enjoy.

CHAPTER 8
HEALING BONE BROTHS

Benefits of Drinking Homemade Bone Broths

My husband and I discovered the power of homemade bone broths during our first round of Whole30 in 2017 and we've incorporated this healing drink into our regimen ever since. I should say "rediscovered," because bone broth was a big part of my childhood and is still considered a very healing drink in my culture. Broths were a healing culinary treasure passed down from great grandparents to the next generation, and I'm so glad we have brought them back into our kitchen!

Sometimes when you feel like having something more substantial than a beverage, yet you're not hungry enough for solid food, and you're leaning towards something savory versus sweet, broths are your answer. My husband has contributed this section. He believes that a great broth is delicious, simple to make, and always gels in the fridge, which is a sign that it has the right ingredients!

These days, making homemade broth may seem a waste of time given the abundance of boxed, packaged, and canned options available on your grocery shelves, but when you begin to study the nutrition label on any box or can, even the organic "natural" ones, you'll quickly realize why homemade broths are the answer to getting the maximum health benefits without the addition of empty processed foods or chemicals.

The bone broths we included here contain a wide range of nutrients that the body needs, as well as collagen. While collagen in bone broth doesn't directly translate to increased collagen in the human body, it does provide a source of amino acids that the body can use where needed. As for vegetable broth, you receive the benefits of vegetables when you don't feel like eating them raw, such as in a salad. Also, these savory broths are a deeper, more filling consistency than the typical hot drink, due to all of these extracted nutrients; the collagen from animal bone especially ends up giving you a thicker broth. This aspect of broths

makes them good substitutions for that sugary afternoon snack or that morning bagel. And when we respond to our cravings by choosing a delicious healthy food or drink (we like to think broths are truly delicious if you make them with these recipes) then it becomes easier to skip over the unhealthy options.

Broths do require more preparation time up front than the other drinks in this book. Unlike when we steep our tea leaves for five minutes, with broths, we are steeping very different things for much longer to extract the highly nutritious broth from the meat, fat, bones, and vegetables. In essence, making a broth is the first step in making soup. You need a rich delicious liquid as a base, called a stock. The main difference between a stock and broth is that a broth is seasoned, whereas a stock is not. This correlates to the concept of a stock being something that you cook with (since seasoning is a part of the cooking process) and a broth is something you can drink on its own.

The recipes to follow use a mix of fresh ingredients, leftovers, and scraps. That is one of the best things about broths—you can use ingredients that would typically go in the trash. Take a look at the things you often discard while cooking—things like chicken bones, meat scraps, onion peels, potato peels, vegetable pulps, and corn cobs (but only ones you have cut the corn from, not gnawed on!). These things can go into your next broth. Experiment.

A couple of preparation notes before you get started:

1. As we are making a large quantity of hot liquid, take care not to put it immediately into your refrigerator or freezer. It must cool down to less than room temperature first. To expedite the process, simply put some water and ice into your kitchen sink. Once you pour the cooked broth through a strainer into a bowl, put the bowl into the ice water to bring down the temperature of the broth more swiftly. It should not take long before the broth is lukewarm and then safe to put into your refrigerator.

   Or, if you have some broth left over in the freezer, then you can put that frozen broth directly into the bowl with the just-prepared broth to lower the temperature without the ice bath.

2. I use three different preparation methods for the recipes, and each method can be used to make any type of broth. The only thing that will vary is the cooking time; bone broths require a longer cooking time to fully break down the collagen, which is the substance that gives the broth its nice "jelly" consistency when cooled.

Beef Bone Broth in the Instant Pot

Roasting meat bones in the oven before boiling them gives a little more depth of flavor to your broth. Also, I use relatively little salt, as I like to add some additional seasoning when I consume the broth. This may be a shake of soy sauce, a squeeze of lemon, and/or a dash or two of cayenne pepper. For this recipe I am using an Instant Pot, which is essentially a smart pressure cooker. This helps make the broth much faster than cooking on the stove or in a Crock-Pot.

If you don't have an Instant Pot, do not worry; if you have a slow cooker, follow the cooking instructions in the chicken bone broth recipe that follows (page 183). For stove top preparation, bring all ingredients to a boil and then simmer partially covered for at least 12 hours. The longer it goes, the better it will be!

Yields 6–7 cups

Ingredients

2 pounds beef bones, thawed

1 large onion, chopped

2 ribs celery, diced

4 cloves garlic, peeled and crushed

1 teaspoon sea salt

8 cups water

Optional and recommended: a handful of herbs, such as parsley, thyme, or rosemary

Instructions

1. Place the beef bones on a roasting tray and place in an oven pre-heated to 400°F. Roast for 30 minutes.

2. After 30 minutes, places the bones into the Instant Pot.

3. Place the onion, celery, garlic, and salt into the pot on top of the bones.

Continued on next spread . . .

4. Slowly add 8 cups of water (be sure not to fill the Instant Pot past the "max fill" line) then lock in the lid.

5. Set the Instant Pot for "PRESSURE COOK, HIGH" for 2 hours.

6. After 2 hours, let the pressure in the Instant Pot release naturally, about 20 minutes.

7. Vent any remaining pressure and then remove the lid.

8. Strain the contents of the Instant Pot through a sieve into a container for cooling and eventual storage.

Chicken Bone Broth in the Slow Cooker

We eat chicken a couple of times a week, and whenever I have leftover chicken scraps or a rotisserie carcass, I toss them into a ziplock bag in the freezer. When I have about 2 pounds worth, it is time to make some chicken broth.

Ingredients

2 pounds chicken bones

1 large onion, peeled and chopped

2 ribs celery, diced

1 cup carrot pulp (or 2 medium carrots, diced)

2 bay leaves

1 teaspoon sea salt

8 cups water

Optional and recommended: a handful of herbs, such as parsley, thyme, or rosemary

Instructions

1. Place all ingredients except for the water in the slow cooker.

2. Slowly add the water to the slow cooker and put on the lid.

3. Set the slow cooker for 12 hours on LOW setting.

4. Strain the contents of the slow cooker through a sieve into a container for cooling and eventual storage.

Vegetable Broth on the Stove

If you do not consume meat, then you can still get the benefits of broth by going with a completely vegetarian version. This recipe is even vegan and, as a bonus, it takes much less time to make this broth than the meat broths!

Ingredients

1 cup mushrooms, cleaned and halved

2 large onions, peeled and chopped

2 cups celery pulp (or 4 ribs celery, diced)

2 cups carrot pulp (or 4 medium carrots, diced)

1 cup parsley, loosely chopped

6 cloves garlic, peeled and crushed

2 bay leaves

1 teaspoon sea salt

10 cups water

Instructions

1. Place all ingredients except for the water into a large pot on your stove top.

2. Slowly add the water to pot and put on the lid.

3. Turn the stove burner to medium-high to bring the pot to boil.

4. Once a boil has been reached, turn the heat down to low and simmer for 1 hour.

5. Strain the contents of the pot through a sieve into a container for cooling and eventual storage.

CHAPTER 9
BUILDING THE HABIT

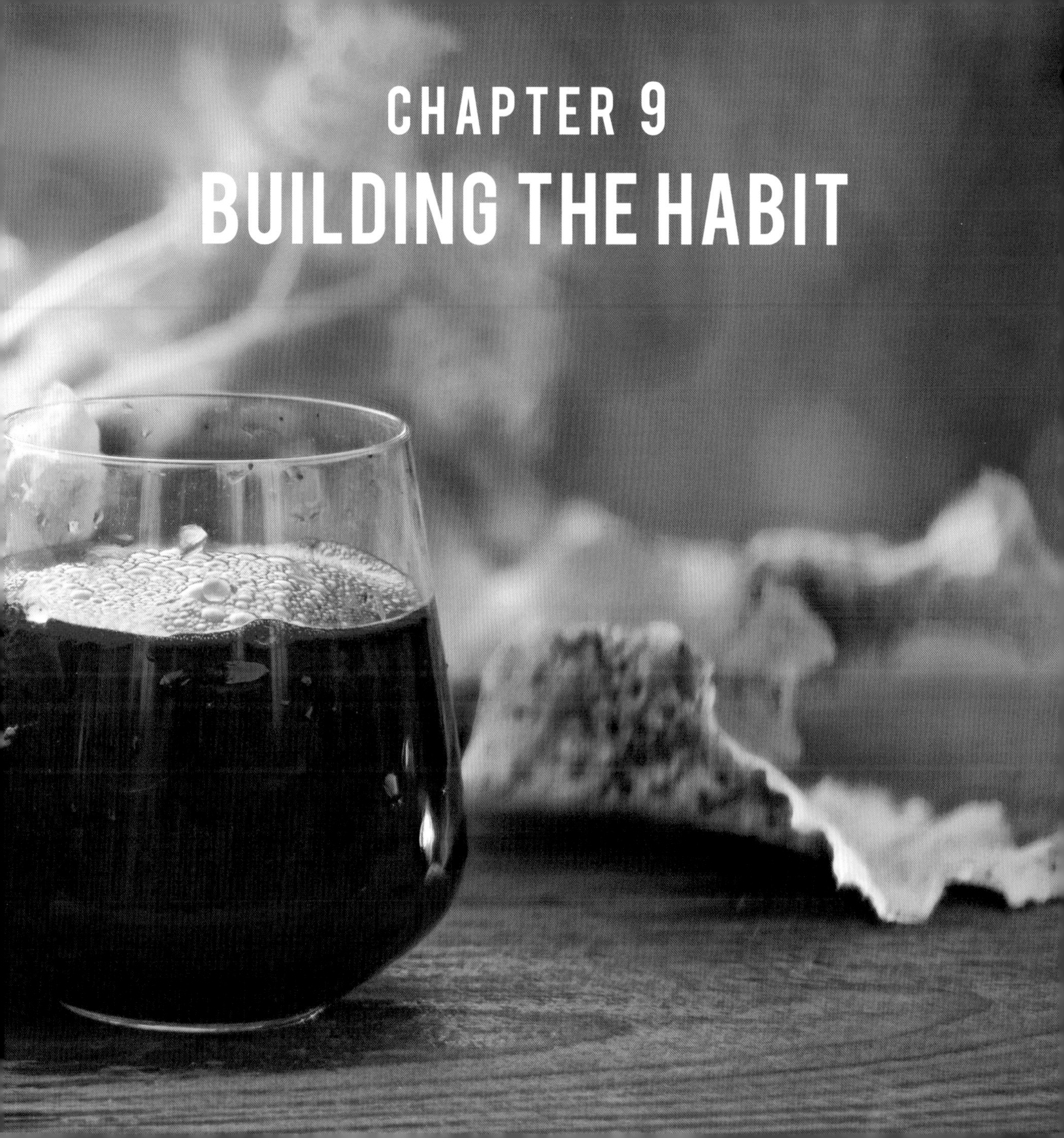

Getting Healthier One Tiny Step at a Time

Whatever phase of life you may be going through now, remember that you are ultimately in charge of your situation. You get to design your own lifestyle; you get to create the grand experience of living and you get to set your own terms and conditions. Your life is not happening to you; it is flowing through you and you are an active participant in that flow. An important part of this grand experience depends on how well you take care of your body, your health, and overall well-being. Whatever path you have fallen into to date is irrelevant as far as your future is concerned. Your past does not dictate your future. At

any moment in time, whether you are eighteen or eighty-one, you can change. You can make new choices. You can develop new habits. You can establish new routines. You can go for better options. And as a result, you can create an enhanced life experience one day at a time. The point is not to live a perfect life from start to finish or to achieve some lofty goal that is way out of reach. The point is to feel good about yourself, your body, and your state of mind, and you can do that by getting healthier one tiny step at a time starting right now. When you feel good in your body, when your state of mind is at peace, you live a happy and fulfilled life from the inside out.

So remember that at any moment, you can move toward a healthier you by taking tiny steps starting now, and that you are worthy of every single step and every big health goal you have for yourself.

I'd like to share one story of my experience on the yoga mat as an example. As I write this chapter at home, we have just arrived back from a vacation in Asia. My husband and I like traveling far and away together, and while it's fun and exotic, it does come with a price. My yoga body has been a wreck for a few days from the plane, train, and car rides and the absence of the daily yoga. Jet lag can be brutal, and it will probably take me a week or so to get back to feeling normal. If I get on my mat the first day back from Asia, expecting a perfect yoga body, I will end up frustrated, disappointed, and even sad. Instead, I temper my expectations and accept that the muscle flexibility can regress even with a short break. I surrender to the reality of what is and then work my way back from there. I gently get back into a breathing and moving practice, expecting nothing, releasing all goals, and simply focusing on being present. I build the practice back up one tiny step—or breath, in this case—at a time.

The best path I have found to achieving long-term goals is to accept where you are and take tiny but consistent steps towards where you want to be. It works wonders.

This process of getting back to where I want my body to be is not necessarily linear, either. Today was the third yoga practice since we got home and I'm about 50 percent of the way back to normal. But the other 50 percent may take another week or two, or even four. So, if it took you, say, a year to get out of shape or gain some extra weight or develop bad health habits, it won't necessarily take you a year to reverse that process. It may take six months or six years. You don't control that. You control your mindset, your actions, and the consistency of those actions,

and you influence—not control—your final outcomes. Obsessing about goals—which then leads to self-criticism, disappointment, and even disillusionment—is the way to failure. Focusing on tiny steps right here and right now is the way to success. Every. Single. Time.

One of the main reasons we get derailed from our goals is this expectation we impose on ourselves of how long it should take us to reach them. How can you possibly know that? You can't. So focus on what you can do. You can have a positive attitude. You can have a healing mindset. You can take consistent daily actions towards your goals. You can remove expectation and celebrate your consistency in taking those actions.

If you have poor eating habits, first, accept where you are, then decide right now that you will create better habits, and then take one teeny tiny step today.

This book has a plethora of ideas for small steps you can take now. Make yourself one healing drink today. If you love it, make it again tomorrow. Set aside five minutes per day toward this activity. Reward yourself at the end of the week. Don't make it a big giant deal if you miss a day. So what? Start back up tomorrow. Start back up again and again if need be. Become a master at starting back up if you mess up. Make it fun and even exciting, and this way, you get over yourself for "quitting" because it wasn't really quitting after all—it was just a little break in your usual routine.

If you adopt one healing drink for a week, celebrate that without measuring the result in how much weight you lost or how much work you still have to do. You're winning. Celebrate what you can do, and then keep doing that. Keep taking tiny steps toward your health every day. The results add up.

In the process of establishing healthy habits, which can last the test of time, small tiny steps consistently always give you greater rewards than massive sudden changes, which often result in an inevitable deflation after the initial excitement.

Can You Be More Specific, Please?

One of the keys to creating a new ritual that will eventually turn into a lifelong habit is to get very, very specific about what you are going to do. Ask yourself: What exactly am I going to do in a new ritual?

Here are some ideas:

1. I will remove one unhealthy drink from my daily routine and it will be my
    ____.
2. I will add one healing shot to my morning routine three times a week,
    Monday, Wednesday, and Saturday and I'll take it at 7 a.m.
3. I will say no to sugary sodas for three days and see how I feel.
4. I will eliminate alcohol from my social life for the next month.

Being specific sends clear signals to your brain as to what it needs to do. Your brain loves specificity and clear instructions. Combine that with a super simple tracking system like a notepad on your phone or an alarm reminder or a journal that you can write in, and you will soon establish a new rewiring in your brain.

Most people have the greatest intention to give up their bad habits or establish new ones, but when it comes down to doing it, they are too general about their goals. They use phrases like "I'll be more careful with my diet" or "I'll eat a little less every day." Those are great intentions, but what do they exactly mean? How is your brain supposed to translate "more" or "less"? Your brain is not getting a clear signal and if you're not 100 percent clear about what you will be doing differently in the face of strongly established habits over the years, you will lose every single time. Being specific—super specific—about your plans is essential here. So remove "more" or "less" from your vocabulary and decide exactly what you commit to doing and then watch how effortlessly it will actually be done.

A Ten-Day Promise to Create a New Habit

You've no doubt heard of the well-known claim that it takes twenty-one days to build a new habit. As my passions grew in the past decade around personal development, health, yoga, fitness, and business, I've broken and re-started loads of habits. For some of us, sticking to something for twenty-one days is too daunting. This is especially true if your resolve to do something is not very strong and you are still—even partially—resisting change.

My intention here for us is to make habit building as easy, effortless, and effective as possible. So I suggest you make an even easier commitment to yourself: Make a ten-day promise to yourself instead of a three-week one. Imagine if all you had to do during the ten days was to *improve* the state of one single health habit? For instance, if your bad habit is an excessive consumption of soda, the new habit would be a lesser consumption. You define what specifically that would look like, because, as we said earlier, being specific is the key to your goals. If your current bad habit is a low consumption of soda, your new habit would be to eliminate soda altogether. If you don't drink soda at all, your new habit would be to add a healing drink to your diet. So on and so forth.

So, to recap your success criteria, first, you are making a type of incremental progress from a current poor habit to a better new habit. Next, you are being very specific about the nature of your progress. You're committing to a very manageable ten-day period. You're taking it one tiny step at a time.

Step-by-Step Habit Change:

1. Decide on the habit that you want to alter for the better.
2. Be specific about the nature of this current habit. For example: I currently drink 5 sodas per day, on average.
3. Decide the improvement factor. For instance, if you want to improve by 50 percent, you will drink 2½ sodas per day on average. Any less would also be acceptable, but more wouldn't.
4. Write it all down. It has been proven that writing down your goals will always impact the results positively. A fantastic resource on this is *Write It Down, Make It Happen* by Henriette Anne Klauser.
5. Make a commitment to yourself with an affirmation: "I commit to going from drinking 5 average sodas per day to drinking 2½ or less sodas per day for ten days starting on _____ date and measuring my results on _____ date."

Repeat the Cycle Again and Again and Again

Since we are making incremental changes, you are at liberty to set the improvement factor as low as you like. However, you'll need to start a new ten-day commitment with a new goal after you finish the first one. This may go on for a while. The idea here is that you let your body decide for you. As you feel better, cleaner, lighter, and more energetic, you may want to increase the improvement factors and make bolder promises to yourself. If you need a break between your ten-day commitments, take one. Think of this as a long-term journey, without a destination in sight, and with the whole purpose of discovering a healthier version of you today than you knew yesterday, knowing that an even healthier version of you awaits you tomorrow.

Making Your Healing Drink Habit Affordable and Efficient

Have you noticed how irrational we can be about money? I've definitely laughed at myself for my own irrational choices. I remember I was in such a hurry to buy our townhome that I couldn't wait an extra day for my Dad—my realtor at the time—to go through with his negotiations. The deal looked fine to me as it was. I wanted the place badly! In the end, he ended up saving us several thousand dollars with no involvement on our part except some patience. Yet, I would spend hours shopping around for the most affordable loose-leaf tea or call up the bank to demand a reversal on a false five-dollar fee from my account or go through great lengths to get a full refund on a twelve-dollar shirt.

I can appreciate the principle of wasting nothing where money is concerned. Still, let me ask you, purely mathematically speaking, is it *really* worth our time to try to save a few dollars here and there, which at best may *may* add up to a few hundred bucks over the course of one's life but for which we pay with high stress, loss of convenience, and waste of precious time and energy? But listen, I'm no saint here. I still lose the higher perspective once in a while and go through lengths to save five dollars! I grew up learning the value of money the hard way and never want to appear wasteful. Yet, as we get older, our values and priorities change, and we may just want to keep in mind that sometimes, our choices may be *an investment* in our time, energy, convenience, practicality, and quality of life, and this type of investment cannot always be measured in dollars and cents.

So while you are seeking to make your habits affordable (for which I'll share some ideas in a moment), remember that you are on a healing journey and you are the master of this operation. Also, you are worth every investment you choose to make in yourself. The rewards of healing your mind and body for longevity are

immeasurable, and on that journey, avoiding stress and inconvenience can be a worthwhile goal.

So ask yourself: How can I make the habits of my healing journey as easy and stress-free as possible for my needs and my lifestyle? How can I make my beverage preparations simple and accessible? And where might I choose to take intentional shortcuts (say, buy packaged nut milk once in a while versus making it at home) because I prefer to be hassle-free and stress-free?

This is your journey. These are your habits and they need to integrate into your life. What I want you to know is that your healing is possible and it can fit your lifestyle. As long as you go about your healing journey in a way that is sensible, practical, and accessible to you, you can make it sustainable over a long period and when you do that, you are winning, dear one. You are winning in life and in health.

Now, about those ideas I promised earlier. In the last twelve years of making juices, smoothies, healing drinks, and healthy foods—with many exceptions and stops and breaks along the way, mind you—I've accumulated a list of ideas on how to make this process affordable, fast, and efficient.

Seven Ideas for Greater Efficiency

1. Invest in some mason jars and some airtight glass preserving jars. You will use them to store your smoothies, nut milks, and juices. Organization is a big key to efficiency.

2. Decide how frequently you will juice. While fresh-squeezed juice is best when consumed right away, you *can* store your juice in airtight glass preserving jars for up to three to five days and still get the benefits. Also, line the pulp bin with a grocery bag for quick cleanup.

3. Make multiple juice recipes in batches. If you have a masticating juicer, you can just run some water through the juicer in between different juice recipes. This can save a lot of time that would otherwise be spent taking the juicer apart to wash it and put it back together.

4. Make smoothies in batches and store them for up to 48 hours in glass mason jars. I find that citrus fruits in smoothies (with the exception of

lemon and limes) don't do well in the fridge, so drink those right away, but otherwise, your smoothie will be fine in the fridge for up to two days.

5. Always keep your juicer and blender on the kitchen counter. If at all possible, make room for these two appliances on the counter so you don't have to take them out and put them away every time you want to use them.

6. Ask for help. If you have a partner, and you are strapped for time, invite them to help with set-up or cleanup or even just with helping you make

decisions. If you are too "independent" to ask for help, get over it fast! Asking for help is a sign of brilliance and smarts, not to mention courage, and you have it all in abundance.

7. Put your healing commitments on the calendar, just like your other tasks. You put your appointments with doctors and clients on the calendar, right? Well, think of this as making an appointment with yourself. Put it on the calendar!

Six Ideas for Greater Affordability

1. Buy what's in season, and if it can be frozen, buy it in bulk, but keep in mind the shelf lives. The denser fruits and vegetables like apples, root vegetables, and zucchini have a longer shelf life in the fridge than leafy greens. With the leafy greens, the thicker leaves like Swiss chard, kale, and collard greens last longer than thinner leaves like spinach, cilantro, or lettuce.

2. Forget about going organic all the way. Organic produce cost can add up fast. Go for what's affordable and fresh. Learn how to pick out the freshest fruits and vegetables. Freshness is the most important factor in taste and quality of your healing drinks.

3. Choose vegetables and fruits that give you the best bang for your buck. These below yield a lot of juice:

   - Apples
   - Lemons
   - Limes

- Oranges
- Celery
- Carrots
- Sweet potatoes
- Beets
- Romaine lettuce
- Cucumbers
- Tomatoes

4. Use frozen fruits for smoothies whenever possible; they are more affordable and last longer. Either buy frozen or freeze your own. Here are fruits that can be frozen: all berries, pineapple, peach, avocado, mango, fig, and banana. I would not freeze apples, kiwi, grapes, melons, or pears.

5. Skip the premium priced juices at Whole Foods or smoothies at fancy health bars. You can make the same drinks at home for less than half the cost, so unless convenience is more important than cost at the time, save your money and make it at home.

6. Skip the "superfoods" that smoothie recipes call for or use what you have, but there is absolutely no need to invest in fancy "superfoods" even if some of my recipes call for it. You can always skip them, as they are never a main ingredient. Superfoods include but aren't limited to goji berries, hemp seeds, spirulina, maca powder, açaí packs, matcha tea, or fancy protein powders.

CHAPTER 10
CONCLUSION AND NEXT STEPS

Closing Thoughts for Your Healing Journey

If I had one wish for you, it would be to begin, just begin. Begin the healing journey and see where it leads you. If you took away a single idea or one new insight from this book, consider it a step toward that beginning. Your ideas of health and healing will evolve and grow over time, as mine have, but for any of that to happen, you must begin.

When I first started out my healing journey in 2007, I had no idea where it would lead me. All I knew is that I'd discovered juicing and felt on top of the world. Juicing was the answer to everything at the time, but as I look back, I see that it was the first of many steps on the healing journey. As I looked closer at my habits and my diet, I realized I'd been kidding myself about some stuff. For instance, I thought I was only having one or two espresso shots a day. When I tracked it, I averaged about 4.3! I was certain I had my meal portions under control, but when I paid more attention, I noticed that I was overeating slightly but consistently. Total honesty with yourself without judgment can be a huge motivator to kick-start your healing and keep it going.

In this book we've talked about breaking down bad habits in tiny but consistent steps. We talked about embracing the healing process, and inspiring your own wellness. We talked about the importance of the healing mindset, how you think and identify with your foods and drinks, and how that mindset can shift to one that can serve you, not harm you, over the long term. We talked about the power of small changes and good choices, both of which you are fully capable of making right now. We talked about the importance of hydration therapy and consuming healthy beverages. As we shared ideas and recipes of many healing drinks with you, we hope that your eyes lit up, your face brightened, and your mouth watered a little at the juice, smoothie, tonic, or elixir recipes. They all await to delight your senses. We wrapped up by talking about building sustainable health habits in tiny steps and taking the excuses out of the equation so that you are set up for success. We talked about ways to create more efficiency and affordability on the journey so that your healing is always within your reach.

May you feel as supported, guided, and inspired as we had set out to make you. It is now all up to you to begin, to take that first step, and to start a new chapter of your life. Raise your health and wellness to newer levels by raising a glass of healing drink and toasting yourself. We wish you much fun, success, and joy along the way.

CHAPTER 11
PRAISE FOR THE TOP BRANDS

As with **The Healthy Smoothie Bible**, I knew I had some favorite brands in mind to recommend, and to do this, I felt it necessary to test and experiment with the products in depth. To that end, I sent out a few inquiries asking for samples from these great companies, and we were blown away by their generosity. Some of these brands are mentioned in the book. We are so grateful to the comprehensive list below for their support of the book's overall mission, discovering your healing journey through smart nutrition and self-care and body awareness. We thank them for being responsive and generous and supplying us with free products to test.

- Arbonne
- Full Leaf Tea Company
- Manitoba Harvest
- Naked Nutrition
- Numi Tea
- Nutiva
- Ora Organic
- Plum Deluxe
- Republic of Tea
- Soul Organics
- TeaMalchi
- Tea Thyme (Orangeburg, SC)

Conversion Charts

METRIC AND IMPERIAL CONVERSIONS
(These conversions are rounded for convenience)

Ingredient	Cups/Tablespoons/Teaspoons	Ounces	Grams/Milliliters
Fruit, dried	1 cup	4 ounces	120 grams
Fruits or veggies, chopped	1 cup	5 to 7 ounces	145 to 200 grams
Fruits or veggies, puréed	1 cup	8.5 ounces	245 grams
Honey, maple syrup, or corn syrup	1 tablespoon	0.75 ounce	20 grams
Liquids: cream, milk, water, or juice	1 cup	8 fluid ounces	240 milliliters
Salt	1 teaspoon	0.2 ounces	6 grams
Spices: cinnamon, cloves, ginger, or nutmeg (ground)	1 teaspoon	0.2 ounce	5 milliliters
Sugar, brown, firmly packed	1 cup	7 ounces	200 grams
Sugar, white	1 cup/1 tablespoon	7 ounces/0.5 ounce	200 grams/12.5 grams
Vanilla extract	1 teaspoon	0.2 ounce	4 grams

LIQUIDS

8 fluid ounces = 1 cup = ½ pint

16 fluid ounces = 2 cups = 1 pint

32 fluid ounces = 4 cups = 1 quart

128 fluid ounces = 16 cups = 1 gallon

Index

Notes

Notes

Notes